What could be more important—and exciting—than helping your child start a relationship with God? *FaithLaunch* shows you how to hide God's Word in your child's heart, leading to genuine heart change. Your whole family will grow closer to the Lord, and each other, when you plug these easy-to-use activities into your next 90 days.

—DR. GARY SMALLEY
Author of *Change Your Heart, Change Your Life*

Transferring a strong faith to our children's hearts cannot be sub-contracted to the spiritual professionals at church or at our Christian schools. Parents must lead the charge. Now you can—with calm and confidence. *FaithLaunch* empowers parents to articulate a clear understanding of the Christian faith to their kids and makes it easy for them to make that faith their own.

—DR. TIM KIMMEL
Author of *Raising Kids for True Greatness*

Spiritually speaking, we're in danger of losing the next generation. Parents are on the front line of that battle. Just in time, here comes *Faith-Launch*—a new way to introduce your kids to authentic faith. Instead of boring your family with lectures, use this book to bond through games and discussions and snacks. Your relationship will grow, and so will your opportunities to introduce your children to the Lord.

D0113584

—JOSH D. MCDOWELL
Author and speaker

FAITHLAUNCH

FAITHLAUNCH

*A Simple Plan to Ignite
Your Child's Love for Jesus*

Tyndale House Publishers, Inc., Carol Stream, Illinois

FaithLaunch

A Focus on the Family book published by Tyndale House Publishers, Carol Stream, Illinois 60188

Focus on the Family and the accompanying logo and design are trademarks of Focus on the Family, Colorado Springs, CO 80995.

FaithLaunch is a trademark of Focus on the Family.

TYNDALE and Tyndale's quill logo are registered trademarks of Tyndale House Publishers, Inc.

John Trent is represented by the literary agency of Alive Communications, Inc., 7680 Goddard St., Suite 200, Colorado Springs, CO 80920, www.alivecommunications.com.

All Scripture quotations, unless otherwise indicated, are taken from the *Holy Bible, New International Version*®. NIV®. Copyright © 1973, 1978, 1984 by International Bible Society. Used by permission of Zondervan Publishing House. All rights reserved. Scripture quotations marked (NIrV) are taken from the *Holy Bible, New International Reader's Version*®. Copyright © 1996, 1998, by International Bible Society. All rights reserved throughout the world. Used by permission of International Bible Society.

Cover design by Jennifer Ghionzoli
Cover photographs copyright © by Veer. All rights reserved.

Library of Congress Cataloging-in-Publication Data
Trent, John.
   Faithlaunch : a simple plan to ignite your child's love for Jesus / John Trent and Jane Vogel.
     p. cm.
ISBN-13: 978-1-58997-531-6
ISBN-10: 1-58997-531-6
   1. Christian education—Home training. 2. Christian education of children. 3. Family—Religious life. I. Vogel, Jane. II Title.
   BV1590.T685 2008
248.8'45—dc22

                 2008010600

Printed in the United States of America
1 2 3 4 5 6 7 8 9 / 13 12 11 10 09 08

CONTENTS

PART I

LAUNCHING YOUR CHILD'S FAITH

by John Trent, Ph.D.

You've never been so nervous in your life.

The relentless Florida sun glints off the crystal of your wristwatch as you glance at it for the thousandth time. Didn't you see these numbers, 11:04 A.M., half an hour ago? History is crawling forward. Half of you wants it to speed up, but the other half wants the clock to stop entirely.

Your stomach grips again as you squint into the distance. For nearly four hours your son has been perched on top of the otherworldly object that towers like a white-and-rust castle against the sapphire sky.

You swallow, and wait. And wait.

Finally your watch tells you that, from now on, things are going to be happening quickly. You can't see most of them from where you are. If that's a blessing, it doesn't feel like one.

Then comes a voice from the PA system. "T minus 30," it says.

The voice sounds too calm. You know the countdown has just passed the point of no return.

Your breathing goes on hold. Numbness starts in your legs and rises like smoke.

"T minus 15," says the voice.

Thousands of gallons of water cascade under the launchpad to muffle the roar and shock waves of the main engines.

"T minus 10."

Something resembling sparklers flashes to life. *Is this supposed to happen?* You feel your torso trembling.

"There go the igniters," says one of the relatives on your left, a burly man from Alabama whose name you can't remember. He doesn't sound concerned. You would breathe a sigh of relief, if you could breathe at all.

"T minus 9 . . . 8 . . . 7 . . ."

You can't remember your own name either now. Your mind is too full of your son's face, the one in his third-grade school picture with the half-combed hair.

"We're ready for main engine start!" says the voice from Mission Control.

At this point, there should be a roar and then a rush of flame that instantly turns the water into billowing steam.

But instead there's . . . silence.

No liftoff. No reaching for the stars.

Nothing.

The astronauts have been dressed for the part. The space shuttle and booster rockets look great on the outside.

But no one loaded any fuel into the tanks, or linked the computers, or actually made any preparations to send your son into space.

Everyone had great intentions.

But it's a failure to launch.

Unfortunately, in too many homes of parents who know and love Jesus, that picture closely resembles what happens when kids grow up and are ready to "launch out" on their own.

Depending on which study you want to quote, anywhere from 50 to 70 percent of children from evangelical Christian families won't embrace the faith as their own when they leave for college. That's tragic. When it comes to faith transference, we're losing the next generation.

Let me shoot straight: It's not the churches' fault. I think the level of ministry excellence in churches today—for the two hours or so that a family is in the building—has never been higher! The music and PowerPoint presentations and kids' and youth programs are *light years* ahead of where they've been in the past. Yet more and more young people are never getting off the launchpad when it comes to personally accepting Christ and growing in their faith.

Here's one reason why.

Recently I asked several hundred parents of younger children at a large church three questions.

1. "Do you think it's important to pass down your faith to your children?" As you might expect, more than 90 percent said, "Yes! It's very important!"

2. "Do you think your child will have a strong faith when he or she gets out of college?" Again, 90 percent of those responding said, "You bet!"

3. "Outside of going to church, what are you doing intentionally to introduce and build a growing faith in your child?" Fewer than 30 percent were doing *anything* purposefully to meet that goal during the 166 hours a week their children were at home.

Think about that. These wonderful, godly, well-intentioned parents strongly believed they should be involved in their children's faith development. They also were highly confident that their children would embrace the faith by the time they were on their own. But when it came to actually preparing their kids, they were just dressing them up and dropping them off at church—and setting themselves up for a failure to launch.

But that doesn't have to be true in your home.

Now is the time for you to realize the incredible impact you can have on your child, helping him or her come to Christ and grow in that relationship. You can do it!

It's not rocket science to help your child reach God's best for his or her life. It's small things, like the fun and incredibly helpful activities you'll learn in this book. They'll go a long way toward filling up those boosters that lift your son or daughter into a lifelong faith.

THE LAUNCH WINDOW IS NOW

Maybe you've heard the statistics. Researchers agree that most people who receive Christ as Savior do so when they're children. One study claimed that 85 percent of born-again Americans launched their faith between the ages of 4 and 14; another survey put the number at 83 percent.[1] The Barna Group's findings in 2004 weren't quite so extreme, with 43 percent becoming Christians before age 13 and 64 percent before age 18.[2]

No matter which numbers are correct, the message to parents has seemed clear enough: Now's the time for you to invest in your child coming to faith. And the best place for that to happen is right in your home. In fact, the same Barna survey found that half of those who received Christ by age 12 did so at the prompting of their parents, with an added 20 percent following the lead of another relative or friend.

No matter how wonderful your church may be, most successful launches happen at or near home. That doesn't have to scare you, even if you're a first-generation Christian like me. I didn't grow up in a Christian home, so I never saw anyone model faith transference. My wife, Cindy, didn't see an active, growing faith displayed in her home, either.

Yet both our children know and love the Lord today, as one finishes graduate school and the other gets ready for college. We truly believe it's because we did—without knowing how or why—many of the things you'll find in this book.

I only wish Cindy and I'd had *FaithLaunch* when we were raising our two precious daughters! We stumbled into many of the things you'll learn in the pages that follow. You don't have to stumble; these resources are tremendous!

Cindy and I didn't "launch" our relationship with Christ when we were children. Our own stories prove that children can accept the Lord when they're at voting age or older. So if your older child doesn't respond to God's invitation before adulthood, the story may be far from over.

Still, the benefits of following Jesus begin in this life. Since you want the best for your child, you want him or her to start receiving those benefits as soon as possible. Children face more challenges today than ever, and at a younger age; introducing them to Christ now, while they're young, is the most important gift you can give them.

It will be an incredible blessing to you as well. The aging apostle John said this about his spiritual children: "I have no greater joy than to hear that my children are walking in the truth" (3 John 4). That's true for any parent of older or grown children who sees them making good decisions and living a life of faith and love for Christ.

WE ALL NEED A LIFTOFF

When it comes to launching your child's faith, strong-arming isn't an option. But neither is sitting on the sidelines, hoping your child will somehow sort it all out alone. So what do you do if you're new to the faith—or, like Cindy and me, have no spiritual road maps from your past to follow?

You could just hope for the best. Like Larry.

Larry didn't know where he was going. He and his passengers were supposed to end up at a restaurant called the Stagecoach Inn, but he didn't know how to get there.

Fortunately, Larry's new car had GPS—the Global Positioning System. By punching a button on the dashboard and speaking the name of his destination, he could display directions on the miniature screen. He'd get there in no time, and impress his passengers to boot.

"Stagecoach Inn," Larry commanded. The others leaned forward, peering at the screen.

Sure enough, a message appeared. It was the name of a local radio station, which proceeded to play some annoying music.

Frowning, Larry tried again. "Stagecoach Inn," he repeated.

This time the GPS came up with an actual destination. Unfortunately, it was a movie theater. In a different town.

After a few more tries, Larry gave up. He found the restaurant the old-fashioned way—by driving until he saw a sign that said STAGE-COACH INN.

Things worked out okay for Larry, other than failing to impress his passengers. But not knowing where you're going when you're launching a rocket—or a child's faith—isn't a wise strategy. It's an invitation to leave your child's faith on the launching pad.

So where do you begin?

First, keep in mind that we're not just talking about getting your child to say some words that he or she doesn't understand or fully believe. For example, Marilyn's parents seemed satisfied when they coached her to pray the "sinner's prayer" at age five. Her mother hugged her, calling it a "great moment" in the girl's life—and it certainly seemed like it was! She'd said the "right" words, after all.

Marilyn's parents must have felt their primary duty was done. From there it was just a matter of sending their daughter to Christian school and church camp and making sure she got on her church's Bible quiz team.

But Marilyn's heart wasn't in this journey. Her interest in Christianity had begun and ended with that prayer. By the time she was a teenager, she hated her life. Today she's turned her back on the "fundamentalism" of her childhood, vowing to spend the rest of her days learning to "be herself."[3]

As Marilyn's story demonstrates, the goal of faith-launching is to cultivate an eternal, personal relationship with God. It's not just to get our child to say words that make us relax or feel better.

That's not to say that "praying the prayer" or having a specific "launch day" isn't important. The act of believing in Jesus, wanting forgiveness for sins, and saying so is an indispensable beginning.

But ignoring the rest of the flight plan can lead to shortcuts that endanger your "astronaut." Parents who aim only to hear the "right words" from a very young child may be tempted to "get this out of the way" as if it were an awkward talk about the birds and the bees. They may fail to supply their kids with enough information as they grow up to make a real, lasting choice. To use a more biblical word picture, they may build a house on sand, not rock.

LAUNCHPAD JITTERS

"Hey," you might say. "Aren't you supposed to be *encouraging* me? I'm already nervous about this faith-launching stuff, and you're just telling me all the things that can go wrong."

Sorry. If you're anxious about helping your child become a Christian, it's understandable. You may think it's all up to you. You may think that if you "fail," the launch window will slam shut and no one will ever be able to reach your child.

Or perhaps you're more worried about how this process might affect your relationship with your son or daughter. What if your child rejects you for acting "weird" when you try to bring up "spiritual things"? What if he or she won't "go along" when you ask for a decision about following Jesus? Will things get awkward—or worse?

Let's look at seven common faith-launching worries parents face—and why you don't have to feel overwhelmed by them.

1. *I'm not an expert on Christianity.* Good! That means you'll be able to talk with your child in plain English, not theological jargon. If you don't quite grasp concepts like the Trinity and original sin, relax. *FaithLaunch* describes them as simply as possible so that you can do the same for your child.

2. *My own relationship with God isn't going too well.* If you believe the basics—that we can receive forgiveness by placing our faith in Christ—you're qualified to address the subject with your child. It's important to deal with your doubts, disappointments, and temptations with the help of a pastor or other mature believer, but waiting for perfection isn't necessary. In fact, you might even find *FaithLaunch* to be a faith-builder for you.

3. *My kid has the attention span of a Chihuahua on caffeine.* Are you afraid of boring your child? Whether the cause is ADHD or just too many video games, a short attention span doesn't have to torpedo your takeoff. *FaithLaunch* features a wide variety of brief activities, not a bunch of lectures. You can take things at your child's pace, and in bite-sized pieces.

4. *I'm no teacher.* Fortunately, *FaithLaunch* isn't a class. It's a series of Family Times—kind of a cross between game night, a devotional, and baking cookies together. You're the leader, but there's no standing at a chalkboard and delivering a memorized lesson. It's as natural as spending time with your child to play with the cat, listen to a song on the radio, or work together on a model plane.

5. *I have to do this alone.* If you're a single parent, or if you're married but your spouse is reluctant to help, you may need to lead *Faith-Launch* as a team of one. No, make that two: God knows all about your

situation. The Family Times have been prepared with you in mind; you won't be required to do anything a mom *or* dad can't do. If you really need flesh-and-blood support, though, you might consider inviting a friend and his or her child to join you for Family Times.

6. *My kid doesn't seem interested in God.* If you haven't talked with your child much about faith before, suddenly immersing yourselves in the subject may seem jarring. You may assume your child isn't interested, yet it's likely he or she has questions but hasn't raised them. Rather than leaping headlong into *FaithLaunch*, you might prepare your child for a couple of weeks beforehand by occasionally asking questions of your own ("Who do you think gave that caterpillar all those legs?") and mentioning your own faith ("I'll be sure to pray about your spelling test tomorrow").

7. *I'm afraid I'll do it wrong and I'll never have another chance.* The good news is that there are a million ways to do it right. Blend *Faith-Launch* with your personality, your child's interests, your family's schedule, your home's layout, your favorite snacks. Share the truths in your own words, and let your child respond without insisting on the "right" answer. Count on the all-powerful God to use your less-than-perfect efforts—in His own time. When it comes to launch windows, He's able to open a lot more than doors.

ONE WAY, MANY FLIGHT PLANS

A space shuttle launch is no haphazard affair. Firing the main engines, for example, doesn't take place "shortly" before liftoff. It happens at *precisely* T minus 6.6 seconds.[4]

Fortunately for us parents, the faith-launching process isn't run by NASA. Introducing your child to Christ isn't bound by stopwatch, formula, technique, or checklist. The only way to God is through faith in Jesus (John 14:6), but there are many ways to launch that faith.

Authors Craig and Janet Parshall recall the varying paths to belief that their children took:

> Looking back at our own children, we're thrilled to remember how they invited Jesus Christ into their hearts in different ways and at different times. Most were at home; one was on a family vacation. Our two daughters responded directly to our own presentations of how to begin a relationship with God; our oldest son was led to the Lord by his sister.
>
> Our youngest son, Joseph, had still another story. He seemed very interested in the gospel and listened carefully as the plan of salvation was explained to him at bedtime one night. Looking down into his big, brown eyes, we told him about God's unconditional love.
>
> How we wanted this little one to know and experience God! We knew that what he was hearing could change his life forever, and his choice would have eternal ramifications. Pretty big stuff for a seven-year-old!
>
> His response: "I want to think it over."
>
> For us, it was an anguished moment. Somehow we resisted the temptation to coerce a confession of faith from this precious person, and respected his need to make an authentic decision for Christ.
>
> The next morning our son walked into the kitchen—and promptly announced that he was ready to invite Jesus into his heart! God heard our silent hallelujahs, even if our son couldn't.[5]

As the Parshalls point out, "Each of our children's decisions for Christ was preceded by slow, consistent teaching about Jesus that occurred in a variety of settings—during car trips, at the dinner table, in Sunday school, at bedtime, and on nature hikes. We found that all of life is an opportunity to share the love of Christ with our children."[6]

In other words, faith-launching takes many forms. The question is: Which forms are right for you?

SPUR-OF-THE-MOMENT VS. STRUCTURE

Michael and Cheri are putting all their eggs in one basket when it comes to helping their five-year-old son, Cooper, launch his faith. The basket is their church; they're counting on Sunday school and Vacation Bible School to do the job. One of these days, they hope, they'll get a call from one of Cooper's teachers, saying he prayed to receive Jesus when an invitation was given.

Alberto and Consuela, meanwhile, have heard a lot about "teachable moments." They can see the value of seizing spontaneous opportunities to tell their eight-year-old daughter, Elena, more about God. Just the other day, for instance, Consuela found Elena watching a cartoon that featured a pair of wisecracking angels. Consuela sat down and watched, too. Afterward, mother and daughter talked about what angels were really like—and why the Bible is a better source of information on the subject than Saturday morning TV is. Alberto and Consuela are hoping for enough teachable moments to tell Elena everything she needs to know to accept Christ.

Patti and Dontrell prefer to plan ahead. At least three nights a week they talk about a Bible verse at the dinner table with their kids, Tyrell and LaTricia. A few months ago Patti and Dontrell decided to invite Tyrell, 6, to receive Jesus as Savior. They even rehearsed the conversation they'd have with him. They breathed a sigh of relief when he said yes. Already they're planning a similar talk with LaTricia, 4—and are praying that she'll be ready.

So which couple is taking the "right" course?

Michael and Cheri aren't wrong to think that one of Cooper's teachers might lead their boy to Christ. But it's hardly a sure thing. And the 120 hours a week they spend with him provide far more opportunities than the 2 hours he spends in Sunday school and children's church. At the very least, they're an important part of Cooper's "launch team."

Alberto and Consuela are wise to act on the biblical direction to "impress [these commandments] on your children. Talk about them when you sit at home and when you walk along the road, when you lie down and when you get up" (Deuteronomy 6:7). Making the most of teachable moments is natural and effective. Still, few of us would rely only on "serendipity" to teach our kids about tying shoes or using a fire extinguisher. Will enough of those moments arise for Elena?

Patti and Dontrell know the value of planning. They aren't afraid to set aside time for discussing spiritual issues, to make sure those aren't lost in the shuffle. They want to turn their priorities into practices. They've read the words of Jesus: "As long as it is day, we must do the work of him who sent me. Night is coming, when no one can work" (John 9:4). They need to watch and listen to Tyrell and LaTricia to make sure that helpful structure doesn't become a controlling cage. But so far unconditional love has kept rules from ruining the relationship.

When it comes to faith-launching, what's the best mix of spontaneity and scheduling? That depends on your family. If you prefer the former, you may need less preparation—but enough to think on your feet, responding to the moment. You won't have to interrupt family routine, which helps your child understand that spiritual things are a natural part of life.

If you're more comfortable with structure, you won't have to wait for teachable moments only. You can ensure covering the most crucial points; you can pick times and methods that fit you and your child;

you can ask for a specific response to the Good News of Jesus, even if the question doesn't "just happen" to come up.

How do you strike a balance between improvisation and intentionality? That's where *FaithLaunch* comes in.

THE FAITHLAUNCH ADVANTAGE

FaithLaunch isn't the only way to introduce your child to Jesus, of course. But it's a good way to do it without pressuring your child, exhausting yourself, or upending your family's schedule. Each of the 13 "Family Times" takes about 30 to 45 minutes; that's 30 to 45 minutes of togetherness, not tedium. You might use one Family Time each week for 90 days—or bits and pieces over a longer period. You get to decide, because *FaithLaunch* is flexible.

The goal is to prepare your child to begin a relationship with God. You'll explore questions like these:
- Who is God, and how does He feel about me?
- Who am I, and why am I here?
- Why do we need forgiveness?
- What's the Bible for?
- Who is Jesus, and what did He do for me?
- How can I join God's family?
- What's heaven like?
- What does God want me to do now?

Since so many children receive Christ as Savior when they're 4 to 7 years old, each Family Time is written with that age group in mind. But shifting gears for kids ages 8 to 12 is easy; just use the optional activities.

FaithLaunch gives you plenty of fun ways to learn, including three *Adventures in Odyssey* episodes to listen to. You'll sculpt with clay, stage a treasure hunt, even tell a story with the help of your child's action figures or dolls. If you need an excuse to play with your child, here it is! And if you need permission to talk about what's important, that's here, too.

The plan for each Family Time is easy to follow. Your goal is clear, and the items you'll need are listed—right down to snacks you might enjoy. To boost your confidence, things you might say are spelled out in bold type—with answers to questions in parentheses. And you're *always* free to adapt the plan to fit you and your child.

There's a bonus, too—another confidence booster. In Part III of the book you'll find answers to questions your child might ask about God, the Bible, Jesus, joining God's family, and more. So there's no need to panic if your child wants to know something that isn't on the tip of your tongue.

THE BIG QUESTION

But what about the big question—the one you may long to ask your child, the one about being ready to receive Jesus? How does that fit into *FaithLaunch*?

If your child already is part of God's family, *FaithLaunch* is a way to affirm that relationship and cover essential concepts that Sunday school might skip. If your child hasn't prayed to receive Jesus yet, the Family Times provide several opportunities to do so. There's no do-or-die confrontation, but a series of low-key invitations to accept God's loving offer of forgiveness and friendship.

Parents get nervous about extending that invitation, fearing they'll word it clumsily or that their kids will R.S.V.P. with a no. But as Mindy Stoms, a director for the children's ministry at Willow Creek Community Church, points out, "One simple phrase causes a child to fill with joy: You're Invited!"

Why? Because it's personal. "They've been selected. They've been included. Somebody wants them. They've heard about how amazing a party can be, and now the real person planning all this wonderful stuff has said, 'This includes you.' "[7]

Mindy doesn't hesitate to invite children to enter a personal relationship with Jesus. "For many kids, this is a very natural step in their spiritual journey. When they hear that the same Jesus they have learned so much about now wants to be their forever friend, wants to take the punishment for the sin that they have, and wants to help them through all the things they face in their life, and wants to eventually live with them forever in heaven, it's no surprise that many say 'YES!' "[8]

How should you present this invitation? Here's some good advice:

- When your children appear to understand the basics of what Jesus has done for them, simply ask something like, "Do you want to pray and ask God to forgive you and make you His child right now?" Using the phrase "right now" makes it easier for you to ask them later again if they aren't ready yet. . . .

- If you're concerned that your child has "prayed the prayer" without grasping all the theology, remember that children need only understand the main points. Being forgiven and becoming a Christian is not like a contract signing in which you must be careful to read all the fine print. It is the start of a loving relationship—a foundation on which your children can build throughout their lives.

- If your children don't accept Jesus in exactly the same way or setting as you might have envisioned, try not to worry or be disappointed. There is no single "correct" way to come to Jesus. It can happen with you, in church or Sunday school, with a friend, as children are thinking by themselves—anywhere. It might be emotional or matter-of-fact. God wants a unique relationship with each person, and each relationship starts in its own way.[9]

FAILURE TO LAUNCH?

But what if your child *doesn't* respond? Does that mean *FaithLaunch* has failed?

Not at all. You will have laid a foundation on which your later efforts—or another person—can build. If your child doesn't seem to accept the invitation, here are five things to keep in mind.

1. *Don't panic.* One child's response may be obvious, but another's may be hard to detect. Take the four-year-old identical twin boys who heard the Good News about Jesus from their dad one day as the three of them lay on a king-sized bed. Right away one of the boys prayed, asking Jesus to be his Savior. Months later, after hearing nothing on the subject from the other boy, the father asked him during a car trip whether he, too, wanted to pray such a prayer. "I already did," the boy said matter-of-factly, clearly considering it a private matter.

2. *Keep the door open.* You may feel disappointed or anxious if your child doesn't react as you'd wanted. But don't let that come between you. Keep having fun and loving your child without reservation. Don't withhold your approval in the hope of making him "come around." Reissue the invitation from time to time if you like, but don't let it turn into nagging. And remember that if your child thinks it's nagging, it is.

3. *Continue to teach and ask questions.* The more your child knows about God, Jesus, the Bible, and heaven, the more reasons he or she will have to accept the invitation. There's no need to postpone talking about spiritual things until "the big decision" has been made. Keep asking questions, too, about your child's view of God in order to gauge his or her progress on the pilgrim's path.

4. *Look and listen for signs of interest and growth.* "By their fruit you will recognize them" (Matthew 7:16). Is your child more willing to help around the house this year than last? Does he show concern when

a sibling is sick or hurt? Is she interested in befriending the lonely new kid at school, or hearing the story of David and Goliath, or putting a quarter in the offering plate, or waving a branch for the Messiah on Palm Sunday? Be thankful for actions that may flow from a developing faith, even if your child has yet to put that faith into words.

5. *Pray.* If that really were your child in the space shuttle, awaiting a launch that looked as if it might never come, isn't this exactly what you'd do? Your heavenly Father wants that relationship with your child, too. Ask Him to help your child understand and take hold of the love He offers. Don't give up. God didn't give up on you, did He?

THE COUNTDOWN BEGINS

The response is up to your child. First, though, you need to give him or her something to respond to. *FaithLaunch* is ready to help you do just that.

Remember where we started. It's simply not an option today to just dress up your children in "church clothes" and expect that they'll figure it all out while you stay busy elsewhere. Yes, it takes effort—but what an incredible privilege to be on your child's "launch team"!

The Lord is standing by with all the power you need. This book—and many other resources on instilling faith at home, available through Focus on the Family and from ministries like ours at www.strong families.com—can help you every step of the way.

We believe in you, pray God's best for you, and are excited for you to dive into *FaithLaunch.* It's so much fun, and can do so much to fill those booster rockets with God's love and light for your child!

Enjoy the flight!

PART II

FAITHLAUNCH FAMILY TIMES

by Jane Vogel

FAMILY TIME 1

ONE GOD, INVISIBLE

MISSION CONTROL:
Where You're Headed

You'll help your child discover that God is a spirit—the only God, the Creator and source of everything.

COUNTDOWN:
Getting Ready

What could be more exciting than launching and guiding your child in a relationship with God? But if you're like most of us, you find the prospect a little daunting, too. Where do you start? What do you say? How do you introduce your child to Someone you can't even see?

In Family Time 1, we start where the Bible starts: with the account of Creation. What better truth to give your child a sense of God's power and grandeur—and to instill delight in God's handiwork! And we use a picture Jesus Himself gave us to help us understand God as spirit—the wind that moves but can't be seen (John 3:5-8).

Prepare for your time with your child by reading through the plan, and especially praying for the presence and guidance of the Holy Spirit.

1. BLAST OFF:
Getting Started

What you need:
- *an inflated balloon*
- *masking tape (optional)*

Sit at your kitchen table, facing your child. Play a game by blowing an inflated balloon across the tabletop to your child. Let him or her blow the balloon back to you. See how many times you can pass the balloon back and forth.

If you like, mark a "goal line" with masking tape and keep track of "touchdowns." You can play this game with as many family members as are available by blowing the balloon around the table.

Ask: **What made the balloon** (or cotton balls as described in Alternate Flight Plan) **move?** (Your breath.)

Could you see your breath? (Younger kids may say they could see their breath, because they don't necessarily distinguish between their breath and the action it caused. Help them see the difference by asking questions like, "What color is your breath? How big is it? Can you see it, or is it invisible?")

If you can't see your breath, how do you know it's real? (You know it's real because you can see what it does—it moves the balloon/cotton balls.)

ALTERNATE FLIGHT PLAN:
Options for Ages 8-12

What you need:
- *cotton balls*
- *masking tape*
- *timer*

Older kids will enjoy a faster-paced, more competitive game. Make a dividing line down the center of the table with masking tape and put a handful of cotton balls on each side of the line. Set a timer for two minutes. The goal is to blow your cotton balls to the other person's side of the table. Whoever has fewer cotton balls on his or her side when the timer rings, wins. If more than two family members are playing, you can form teams—or divide the table into thirds, quarters, and so on.

2. EXPLORATION:
Discovering Truth

What you need:
- *a Bible*
- *an instrumental (no words) music CD or tape*

Tell your child that together you're going to learn about Someone who's invisible, but who's still definitely real.

Read aloud John 4:24a, pointing out the words to your child if he or she is able to read. Explain that "God is spirit" means that God doesn't have a body, and we can't see Him. But we still can know that God is real, because we see what He does—just as your child could see what his or her breath did when he or she blew on the balloon or cotton balls.

Ask your child if he or she knows anything that God has done. You don't need to prompt any answers; just use the question as a way to find out what your child already knows about God. Then open your Bible to Genesis 1 and read aloud verse 1.

Start playing an instrumental music CD. Explain that you're going to have some fun moving to the music and acting out a true story. You'll give instructions; your child should be ready to "freeze" in position when you give the direction. If your child wants you to move along with him or her, feel free!

Using the following as a guide, paraphrase Genesis 1:1–2:2 and provide instructions. Don't worry about using these exact words; your own will be just fine.

In the beginning, God created the heavens and the earth. The earth didn't have any shape. It was empty. It was dark. Close your eyes and move slowly. Imagine how it would be if everything were very, very dark!

On day 1, God said, "Let there be light." And there was light! Open your eyes and freeze! What a difference it makes when there's light! God saw that the light was good. God called the light "day." He called the darkness "night." You can move again now!

On day 2, God said, "Let there be a huge space." And that's exactly what happened! Make yourself as big as possible, and move with the hugest movements you can! God called the huge space "sky." Stretch up high toward the sky, and freeze! Now unfreeze!

On day 3, God said, "Let dry ground appear." And that's exactly what happened! God called the dry ground "land." He called the waters "oceans." Imagine you're a wave in the ocean. How would you move? Be a wave . . . now freeze! God saw that the land and the oceans were good. You can move again! Then

God said, "Let the land produce plants—trees and flowers and all kinds of plants." And that's exactly what happened! Pretend you're a plant growing up from the ground. How tall will you grow? Grow, and grow, and grow, and . . . freeze! God saw that it was good. Now unfreeze!

On day 4, God said, "Let there be lights in the huge space of the sky." And that's exactly what happened! God made the sun, and the moon, and the stars. Move as if you're a star twinkling in the sky! Now freeze! God saw that it was good. You can move now!

On day 5, God said, "Let the oceans be filled with living things." And that's exactly what happened! Pretend you're a fish. Now an octopus! [Add any sea creatures your child knows.] Now freeze! Okay, unfreeze! God said, "Let birds fly above the earth across the huge space of the sky." And that's exactly what happened! Pretend you're a baby bird just learning to fly. Now you're getting

ALTERNATE FLIGHT PLAN:
Options for Ages 8-12

What you need:
- *Bibles*
- *slips of paper numbered 1 through 7*

Older kids can enjoy exploring the creation account through movement, too, but they probably won't want to move to music with you. Instead, play a version of charades. Take turns drawing a numbered slip of paper and reading silently from the Bible about what God created on that day. While the actor performs the charade, the guesser(s) can look in Genesis 1 for clues as to what day is being represented.

stronger. Now pretend you're a beautiful, strong bird that can fly fast! Now freeze! God saw that it was good. You can move again!

On day 6, God said, "Let the land produce all kinds of animals." And that's exactly what happened! Imagine you're an elephant. How about a monkey? [Add animals your child knows and enjoys.] Now freeze! Last of all, God said, "Let us make people." So He created a man and a woman and He said, "Have babies and take care of this world that I've made." Pretend you're taking care of your favorite animal. Now freeze! God saw everything He had made. And it was very good. Unfreeze!

By day 7, God had finished the work He'd been doing. So on the seventh day He rested. You can take a rest, too!

3. REENTRY:
Bringing the Truth Home

Repeat the main point you want your child to grasp: **God is spirit, so we can't see Him. But we can know He's real because we can see what He's made.**

Take turns naming things that God has made. If weather permits, go outside—or at least look out a window. With young children, reinforce the point by saying each time, **God made _____.** With older children, you can turn this into a game of "I Spy," or take turns naming some of the things you like best in God's creation.

4. SPLASHDOWN:
Applying What You've Learned

Remind your child that on day 6 of creation, God gave people the job of taking care of all that He'd made. Together, choose a way that you and your child can show special care for part of God's creation.

What you choose will depend on your child's age and your living situation. Young children will do best with a single action they can take right away. Here are some examples:
- grooming or checking the food and water for a family pet
- watering a houseplant or an outdoor plant
- scattering birdseed or pieces of bread for birds.

Older kids probably have heard enough about ecology to come up with ways to serve as stewards of God's creation. Some examples:
- setting up or maintaining a family recycling project
- picking a way to reduce energy consumption as a family (lower-wattage lightbulbs, adjusting the thermostat, turning off a CD player when leaving a room)
- picking up litter in a section of park, forest preserve, or roadway.

SPACE SNACK

What you need:
- *"Creation" food (see below)*

Want to wrap up with refreshments? Try a snack that reminds your child of God's creation—like animal crackers, a "solar system" made of fruit "planets" (an orange, a grape, a cherry, a peach, etc.), or "gummy" versions of some of God's creatures (fish, worms, bugs, and bears).

FAMILY TIME 2

WHO LOVES YOU?

MISSION CONTROL:
Where You're Headed

You'll help your child understand that God is three persons: Father, Son, and Holy Spirit. He's also loving, holy, just—and interested in each of us.

COUNTDOWN:
Getting Ready

In Family Time 1, you helped your child understand that God is a spirit. But God isn't an abstract power, like the Force in *Star Wars*. He's personal. And He delights in showing His love to us.

We can't talk biblically about God without talking about the Trinity, one God in three persons: Father, Son, and Holy Spirit. Maybe you've heard object lessons that try to explain how the Trinity "works," comparing God to water in the forms of liquid, steam, and ice—or to three parts of an apple. That's not where we're going in this Family Time. For one thing, young children think concretely; until they reach adolescence, most aren't able to process the abstract ideas in those object lessons. And some of those object lessons tend to depersonalize God.

Theologian Cornelius Plantinga, Jr., in his book *A Sure Thing* (Faith Alive, 1986), offers an analogy that most children can understand: a family. "Think of three persons in a family. They are very much alike. . . . Further, they know each other deeply and love each other. They share memories, experiences, hopes, and plans. If anyone or anything (such as a mugger or a tornado) threatens them, they turn to face this threat together. They are three persons, but one family unit" (p. 21).

No human analogy really can "explain" God. Your goal in this Family Time is simply to help your child discover and embrace the way the Bible speaks of God as Father, Son, and Holy Spirit.

1. BLAST OFF:
Getting Started

What you need:
• *gift bags or gift wrap*
• *small gift items*

Show your child the gifts you've gathered. Let him or her choose one. Put it in a gift bag or wrap it up; label it clearly with his or her name.

Together, select gifts for other members of the family. After wrapping or bagging and labeling the presents, set them aside. Explain that you'll open them later. First you'll be thinking about presents and what they have to do with God.

ALTERNATE FLIGHT PLAN:
Options for Ages 8-12

Young children may be delighted to wrap and unwrap presents, but older kids need an element of surprise. Instead of letting them see the choices, supply a "mystery" bag of goodies; ask their preferences but keep the final choice a surprise.

Depending on the gift items you gather, your questions might include, **Would you prefer something to play with or something to eat? Something sweet or salty? Chewy or hard?** Kids will have the fun of guessing what treat might fit those descriptions.

2. EXPLORATION:
Discovering Truth

What you need:
- *a Bible*
- *plates*
- *modeling clay or dough*

With your child, use the clay or dough to sculpt some tasty-looking food—whatever your child thinks sounds delicious. Put it on a plate. Then sculpt some nasty, scary snakes and bugs, and put them on the other plate.

Open the Bible to Luke 11:11-13. Explain that you'll be reading something Jesus said. Read from a kid-friendly version (*The Message* takes an especially vivid look at this passage) or paraphrase it in your own words. Use your sculptures to illustrate.

Ask:

What kind of mom or dad would give you [whatever favorite food your child sculpted] **for supper?**

What kind of mom or dad would give you snakes and bugs for supper?

What kind of mom or dad is God more like?

Explain that the Bible tells us a lot about how God is like a parent. It tells us about God the Father—and about Jesus, who is God the Son. It also tells us about God the Holy Spirit. Even though the Bible tells us about all three of these Persons, they are only one God—sort of like the way you have one family made up of different people.

ALTERNATE FLIGHT PLAN:
Options for Ages 8-12

With older kids, you can spend a little more time talking about the concept of the Trinity. Have them reread Luke 11:11-13 and identify where each person of the Trinity appears. (Jesus isn't mentioned in the passage because He's the one speaking—see verses 1 and 2.)

Challenge your older child to identify the three persons in the account of Jesus' baptism (Luke 3:21-22); have him or her read about baptizing in the name of the Father, Son, and Holy Spirit in Matthew 28:19.

3. REENTRY:
Bringing the Truth Home

What you'll need:
• *modeling clay or dough*

Help your child focus on the important truths you've talked about by saying something like this:

I want to remember that God is *loving,* **like a good mom or dad. So I'm going to make a heart to remind me of that.** Shape a heart from clay or dough and invite your child to shape one, too.

I also want to remember that God *cares about us.* **He wants to give us good things. I'm going to make a little shape of myself, because God cares about me. You can make a shape of yourself, because God cares about you!**

Let's also remember that there's only *one God* **and the Bible talks about Him in** *three persons*—**Father, Son, and Holy Spirit. I'm going to make a 1 and a 3 to remind me of that. How about you?**

When you and your child are both done sculpting, point to each of the shapes and ask your child to tell you what they remind him or her of.

ALTERNATE FLIGHT PLAN:
Options for Ages 8-12

Instead of telling older kids what shapes to make, list the main truths you'd like them to remember. Ask them to model reminders of their choice.

4. SPLASHDOWN:
Applying What You've Learned

What you need:
• *the presents from the "Blast Off" step*

Open the presents you wrapped earlier and enjoy them. As you do, talk about how you feel about getting gifts, and how you might want to respond to someone who gives you a gift.

Ask your child to think about what he or she would like to say to God about the good things He gives. Then pray together.

SPACE SNACK

What you need:
• *grab bag of treats*

Want to wrap up with refreshments? If the presents you're opening aren't edible, bring out a grab bag of treats and let your child choose—without looking in the bag—two for you and two for him or her.

FAMILY TIME 3

MADE FOR A REASON

MISSION CONTROL:
Where You're Headed

You'll introduce your child to the idea that we're spiritual beings—made in God's image, loved by Him, and created to be part of His family.

COUNTDOWN:
Getting Ready

This time you'll help your child to see that, because we're made in God's image, we too are spiritual creatures. God made us to reflect who He is and to respond in love to Him and to other people.

A lot could be said about what it means to be created in the image of God. If you have older children, you may want to explore the biblical basis for the classic definition of the image of God as "true knowledge, righteousness, and holiness." But if that's more than you and your child are ready to absorb, don't worry about it. Living out who we were made to be—image-bearers of God—is a lifelong process. For today, pointing your child in the right direction is enough!

1. BLAST OFF:
Getting Started

Play a game of "Mirror." Face your child and move slowly, having your child copy your movements as if he or she were your mirror image.

After a while, trade roles so that your child initiates the movement and you play the part of the mirror. You can do this with your whole family at once, either in pairs or with one leader and multiple "mirrors."

Then ask, **When you were my mirror in this game, how were you like me? How were you different from me?**

ALTERNATE FLIGHT PLAN:
Options for Ages 8-12

You can expose older kids to some important vocabulary of the Bible by teaching them the phrase, "the image of God." Introduce the word "image" by saying something like this: **When you look in the mirror, you see your reflection. Another word for a reflection in the mirror is** *image.* **When you were my image in this game, how were you like me? How were you different from me?**

2. EXPLORATION:
Discovering Truth

What you need:
- *a Bible*
- *a balloon (or cotton balls, if that's what you used in Family Time 1)*
- *clay or dough shaped like a heart*
- *a hand mirror*

Tell your child that together you're going to learn about being a mirror (or image) of God. Read Genesis 1:27 and explain that God made people to be like mirrors of Him. (If you're using a translation that uses the word "man" for humankind in this verse, make sure to clarify that the term includes boys and girls, men and women—as the second half of the verse makes clear.)

Tell your child that, just as in the mirror game, we are like God in some ways—and different from Him in other ways.

Show the balloon and help your child remember what you learned about who God is when you played "pass the balloon." (God is a spirit.) Hold up the mirror to your child and say, **You're created to reflect God. You're a spiritual being, too. Even after your body dies, your spirit will live forever. That's one way you are like God.**

Ask, **Does God have a body?** (No.) **Do you have a body?** (Of course!) Turn the mirror facedown and say, **God doesn't have a body, but you do. That's one way you're different from God.**

Show the clay or dough heart and help your child recall that you used the heart to remind you that God cares for us and is a loving Father. Hold up the mirror to your child and say, **You're created to reflect God. He made you to be part of His family.**

Ask, **Are you always good and kind and loving?** (No!) **Is God always good and kind and loving?** (Yes.) Turn the mirror facedown and say, **God is always good, but sometimes we aren't. That's another way we're different from God.**

ALTERNATE FLIGHT PLAN:
Options for Ages 8-12

Ask your child to listen for the word "image" as you read Genesis 1:27 and to identify who is being an image of whom. (Most translations use the word "image" in that verse; check yours before you read.) Point out that God made people in His image—to reflect Him.

As you talk about the fact that people are spiritual beings made to be part of God's family, read together 2 Corinthians 6:18. If you want to dig deeper, explore what the Bible says about the image of God in Ephesians 4:24 (righteousness and holiness) and Colossians 3:10 (knowledge).

3. REENTRY:
Bringing the Truth Home

What you need:
- *table and chairs*
- *stuffed animals, dolls, or action figures*

Make the idea of God's family concrete to your child by creating a "family" at your kitchen or dining room table. Start by saying something like this:

God made us to be part of His family. If you could choose anyone to be in our family, who would it be?

Your child may simply name members of your existing family, or may pick friends or celebrities or even cartoon characters. Ask your child to explain why he or she would like to have those people around.

Then say:

Let's see what kind of "family" we can come up with in just five minutes. You can use anything you can find—stuffed animals, dolls, action figures, or pictures of people. Ready . . . set . . . go!

Let your child take the lead in looking for "family members." When time is up, assemble these "relatives" around the table.

Ask:

Do you notice any family resemblance? (Probably not.) **How do you think these family members would get along with each other? Is this how God came up with His family?** (No.)

ALTERNATE FLIGHT PLAN:
Options for Ages 8-12

Older kids probably won't be interested in collecting a "family" of toys. Instead, ask them to create a message about being made in God's image. The title: "This Is Me." They can present it in any form they like. Some possibilities include:

- a song or rap
- a news broadcast
- a drawing (which they must explain)
- anything else that they propose and you agree to.

Explain that God didn't run around the house grabbing whatever He could find and call it "family." He made each of us to be one of a kind. And He wants to be close to us, to be a Father to us.

In subsequent Family Times, you'll address the question of how a person becomes part of God's family—what some would call the difference between being a *creation* of God and a *child* of God. For now, it's enough for your child to understand that God wants such a relationship.

4. SPLASHDOWN:
Applying What You've Learned

What you need:
- *paper*
- *markers*
- *tape*

Ask:

If you really believe you're created in God's image to be part of His family, how will you feel about yourself? Good or bad?

Most kids probably will say, "Good." If needed, explain that God must value us pretty highly if He wants us in His family. And to be like Him in even a few ways is an honor. To reflect those ideas, create "bumper stickers" to go on a mirror—one for each of you. Each sticker should start with the phrase, "God made me, and . . ."

Technologically inclined kids may want to make theirs on the computer instead of using markers. Come up with your own catchy sayings or choose one of the following:

- God made me, and He doesn't make junk!
- God made me, and He made you, too!
- God made me, and He knows what He's doing!
- God made me, and He's an artist!

SPACE SNACK

What you need:
• *people-shaped cookies (see below)*

Want to wrap up with refreshments? Try something people-shaped—like gingerbread men or cookies you bake (and decorate, if you have time) with your child. If you like, talk about how the cookies are "made in your image."

THE RIGHT TO BE WRONG

MISSION CONTROL:
Where You're Headed

You'll help your child understand that we have the capacity for good and evil and are accountable for choosing to do what's right.

COUNTDOWN:
Getting Ready

When God first made people, there was nothing wrong with them. They reflected God's image perfectly. They were given the job of taking care of the world God had made, and they loved one another as God intended.

But when Adam and Eve rebelled against God, everything changed.

Oh, we still have friends and family members we love. We sometimes act unselfishly to help them. We even give them gifts. But most of the time, the people we care about most are . . . ourselves!

We want to have a good time. We want to do whatever we wish and not have to obey anyone else, including God. We get vengeful and greedy and mean. Since practically everyone acts this way, our world is full of hurt.

As part of this Family Time, you'll listen to an episode of *Adventures in Odyssey* that shows how Connie discovers that people aren't basically good. Even *she* isn't as good as she'd thought!

We're quick to make excuses for our wrongdoing. We blame our friends or say we were having a bad day. But God isn't impressed.

Tell your child the truth. Kids know when they're being mean to someone, when they're being selfish. Chances are that hearing about this side of human nature will come as no surprise.

1. BLAST OFF: Getting Started

Work off some energy by playing a rousing game of Simon Says. Take turns leading and letting your child lead. Afterward, say something like this:

You wanted to make the right moves in this game. Did you always do it? Why not?

How is that like real life? Do you ever want to do the right thing, but end up doing the wrong thing anyway?

What would happen to the game if the leader said it didn't matter if anybody did the wrong thing?

We can do what's right, but we can also do what's wrong. Just like in a game, it matters which we choose.

ALTERNATE FLIGHT PLAN:
Options for Ages 8-12

Older kids can have just as much fun with Simon Says as younger kids do. To keep them involved, make sure the game moves at a fast pace. Up the difficulty level by saying one thing (for example, "Simon says, touch your nose") while doing another (touching your chin, for instance).

If you're playing with only two people, add an element of competition by timing the rounds. If you go longer without messing up, you win; if your child goes longer, he or she wins.

2. EXPLORATION:
Discovering Truth

What you need:
• FaithLaunch *audio CD, tracks 1-3, "Promises, Promises"*
• *CD player*

Get comfortable and listen to the *Adventures in Odyssey* episode "Promises, Promises." This might be a good time to break out some snacks.

3. REENTRY:
Bringing the Truth Home

After listening to the episode, talk about a time when you lost your temper. How do you feel about it now? Then ask:

Can you think of a time when you've gotten mad or impatient at somebody, the way Connie did? What happened?

Connie told Whit that "everybody's basically good deep down inside." Why did she decide she was wrong? What do you think about that?

Whit said, "Mankind has been violent ever since we got kicked out of the Garden of Eden." Do you know what he was talking about? (If your child doesn't understand the reference, summarize the account of Adam and Eve's fall and how Cain murdered his brother Abel [Genesis 3–4].)

Did God say to Adam and Eve, "Oh, well—you did something wrong. No big deal"? Or did it matter?

What kinds of things do we do wrong? Do they matter to God?

What things do you do that are good and right? How do you think God feels about that?

4. SPLASHDOWN:
Applying What You've Learned

If your child is familiar with prayer and is likely to feel comfortable praying, encourage him or her to tell God about the things he or she does wrong and to ask for help in choosing to do what's right. If not, take the lead and pray yourself about how all of us fall short.

In either case, your goal is to acknowledge the reality that we tend to disobey God—and can choose otherwise. If your child has become more aware of the need for forgiveness during this Family Time and has heard before how to receive Jesus as Savior, he or she might pray to do so now. If so, you'll want to affirm this decision. If not, rest assured that upcoming Family Times will address the question of how to ask God's forgiveness and begin a relationship with Him.

SPACE SNACK

What you need:
• *snacks to choose from (see below)*

If you didn't have refreshments while you listened to the *Adventures in Odyssey* episode, you might wrap up by having your child choose between two snacks. Hold them behind your back and ask your child to "pick a hand." To reinforce the point of this Family Time, you could mention that we have plenty of chances every day to choose between right and wrong, too.

FAMILY TIME 5

HOW DO WE KNOW?

MISSION CONTROL:
Where You're Headed

You'll help your child discover that we can know God because He teaches us about Himself in His creation and His Word.

COUNTDOWN:
Getting Ready

Why do you want to launch your child's faith? Why encourage him or her to follow Jesus? Why not introduce your child to some other belief system—or none at all?

It probably has something to do with your trust in what the Bible says. When it comes to information about the supernatural world, it's the Christian's . . . well . . . Bible.

Isn't it amazing that God makes Himself known to us in that

Book? Approach this Family Time with a sense of wonder at God's self-revelation, and your child will catch that awe.

1. BLAST OFF:
Getting Started

What you need:
- *five lunch bags labeled "B," "I," "B," "L," and "E"*
- *nonbreakable objects starting with the letters B, I, B, L, and E (example: ball, ice cream scoop, book, lime, eraser)*

Without your child seeing the objects, put each in the bag with the corresponding letter. Staple the bags shut.

Lay out the bags so that they spell "BIBLE." Challenge your child to guess what's in each bag by handling it but not opening the bag. Explain that the object starts with the letter on the bag. (This game is even more fun if several people are guessing, so involve as many family members as possible.)

After everyone playing has guessed, open the bags and see if any guesses were correct. Then ask:

Which objects were easy to guess? Why?

Which were hard to guess? Why?

ALTERNATE FLIGHT PLAN:
Options for Ages 8-12

With older children, use the words *reveal* and *revelation*. The shape of the objects helped *reveal* what they were; the Bible is God's *revelation* to us; it is one way He *reveals* Himself.

Point out that the shape of the object helped you know about the object—you could see the shape a little, and you could touch it.

Say: **Because God is a spirit, we can't see or touch Him. How can we know about Him?** Affirm as many of your child's answers as you can; then say something like this: **We can know God because He tells us about Himself. Let's see what the Bible has to say about how God lets us know about Himself.**

2. EXPLORATION:
Discovering Truth

What you need:
• *a Bible*
• *a favorite Bible verse or passage about God*

Read aloud Psalm 19:1-4. Help your child understand that the Bible says we can learn about God from nature—the "heavens" or skies, and all the other things God created.

Go outside, find something in nature that can remind you about God, and share it with your child. If you can't go outside or can't find anything "natural," search an appropriate Web site, a nature book, or a picture book that has lots of scenes from nature in it.

What you say will depend on your child's maturity. Young children think concretely; a good example might be an ant or some other tiny thing. You could say something like, **This tiny ant shows me how perfectly God can make even the littlest things. I could never make something this small without smashing it, but God can! If He's so careful in making a tiny ant, I know He must be really careful about taking care of you!**

Next, invite your child to find something to show you and to tell you what he or she can learn about God from it.

Now share a favorite Bible passage with your child—one that describes God or how He feels about us. Here are some possibilities:

- Matthew 10:29-31 (God knows all about us and values us highly.)
- Deuteronomy 4:35 (There is only one God.)
- Psalm 74:12-17 (God is like a king—but so powerful He can control the sea, day and night, sun and moon, and the seasons.)

ALTERNATE FLIGHT PLAN:
Options for Ages 8-12

We learn about God through the Bible, but is what we learn there true? Younger children usually don't raise questions about the Bible's reliability, but some older children may. If your child is wondering why he or she should trust Scripture, you might share the following reasons adapted from the book *Stand* by Alex McFarland (Focus on the Family/Tyndale, 2005).

1. The Bible has been preserved and is indestructible. It's outlived all its enemies. Existing manuscripts indicate that it's been accurately copied through the centuries.

2. There is unity to the Bible. Even though it was written by about 40 individuals over a period of 1,500 years, it contains a consistent message.

3. The Bible is supported by archaeology. Discoveries by archaeologists over the years have shown over and over again that the Bible is accurate in its historical facts.

4. Bible prophecies have predicted the future, sometimes hundreds of years in advance.

Finally, ask your child to tell you a favorite Bible story. Ask: **What does that story help us learn about God?**

If your child doesn't have enough experience with the Bible to name a favorite story, ask: **Can you remember anything about God that came from the Bible and that we talked about during one of our Family Times?** Some examples:

- John 4:24a (God is a spirit.)
- Genesis 1:1 (God created the world.)
- Luke 11:11-13 (God the Father gives us, His children, good gifts.)
- Genesis 1:27 (God made us in His image.)

Wrap up this part of your Family Time with a comment along these lines: **We can know about God through the things He's made—and through His Book, the Bible.**

3. REENTRY:
Bringing the Truth Home

What you need:
- *Bible*
- *large sheet of paper*
- *markers or crayons*
- *tape*

Provide an age-appropriate story Bible, paraphrase, or translation for your child to keep. Write his or her name and the date on the presentation page if there is one. Help him or her make a personalized cover for the Bible, using a large sheet of paper and markers or crayons.

If the Bible has special features such as "fun facts" or devotional readings, point those out. Ask your child to pick a place to keep the Bible so that it doesn't get lost.

4. SPLASHDOWN:
Applying What You've Learned

What you need:
- *letter in envelope*

Before your Family Time, write an encouraging note to your child and seal it in an envelope. Address it to your child and draw a postage stamp on it, but don't include your name or return address.

Ask: **Who do you think this letter might be from? What do you think it's about?**

Challenge your child to figure out the answers to those questions in one minute without opening the envelope. When time is up, let him or her try to guess the sender and the contents. Then have your child open the envelope and read the note (or read it to him or her).

Next, say something like this:

Suppose you got a letter from the President [or Prime Minister]. Note: Very young children may relate better to a letter from Grandma or Grandpa.

What would you do when the letter came? Would you open it and read it (or have someone read it to you), or would you leave it unopened?

How is the Bible like a letter to us from God?

What should we do—open it and read it, or leave it unopened? Why?

As needed, point out that the best way to find out what God wants to tell us about Himself is to open His letter and read it. Take a moment to thank God for making Himself known through nature and through the Bible.

SPACE SNACK

What you need:
* *a treat with honey in it*

Want to wrap up with refreshments? Read Psalm 119:103: "How sweet are your words to my taste, sweeter than honey to my mouth!" Explain that this verse is talking about God's words—the kind found in the Bible. Serve a snack that contains honey; discuss how sweet it is. How could God's Word be sweeter?

FAMILY TIME 6

GONE FROM THE GARDEN

MISSION CONTROL:
Where You're Headed

You'll help your child grasp the fact that our sin separates us from God.

COUNTDOWN:
Getting Ready

Sin messes up our relationship with God. Like Adam and Eve, we're barred from paradise because of our rebellion. Yet we're so used to carrying our tendencies around that we may not even realize how pervasive they are.

In the previous Family Time you made it clear that we don't naturally gravitate toward doing the right thing. This time you'll explain why. Help your child see that Adam and Eve's story is our story; the same sin that drove Adam and Eve from fellowship with God is part of our daily experience.

It's bad news. But we need the diagnosis if we're to realize that we need the cure. The good news is that God hates not just our sin, but the separation it creates between us and Him. And He's willing to take extreme measures to bring us back.

1. BLAST OFF:
Getting Started

What you need:
- *materials for making a model of the Garden of Eden (small plastic building blocks, animal figurines, real or artificial plants, etc.)*
- *a small figure to represent each person participating*

It's creative construction time! Gather materials to create a miniature Garden of Eden with your child. It can be whatever size you like. The goal is to have fun and make your model as awesome as you can.

Depending on your child's interests and the materials on hand, you might use any of the following:
- farm or circus animal figures
- trees and flowers from play sets
- a dirt-filled flowerpot into which you've transplanted plants or inserted cut flowers and twigs
- plants and animals cut from construction paper
- "ponds" made of aluminum foil or water in plastic margarine tubs

If your climate and setting permit, try this project outside. Don't rush; enjoy working on it together, using the time to recall some things you've learned so far about God's good creation.

When you've created your Eden, choose a figure (or model one from clay or foil) to represent each of you. Put the figures in the "Garden."

2. EXPLORATION:
Discovering Truth

What you need:
- *a Bible*
- *modeling clay or dough*

Model one more thing—a snake—out of clay or dough. Put that in the Garden, too.

Read Genesis 3 from a child-friendly translation or children's Bible, or retell the account in language your child will understand. As you tell the story, have your child act it out with the figures in your Garden.

3. REENTRY:
Bringing the Truth Home

Check your child's understanding by having him or her summarize the story for you, using the Garden and figures as props.

Then ask:

What would the world be like if people had never disobeyed God?

How do you think Adam and Eve felt when they got kicked out of the Garden?

How do you think God felt?

ALTERNATE FLIGHT PLAN:
Options for Ages 8-12

If you think your child will see making a model Garden of Eden as a "baby" activity, try doing some "kid on the street" interviews instead. In person or via phone or instant messaging, help your child ask friends and family questions like the following:

Who lived in the Garden of Eden?

Who was created first—Adam or Eve?

What kinds of fruit were okay to eat in the Garden?

Which kind wasn't? Why?

Why did Adam and Eve eat it anyway?

What happened then?

What does this story have to do with us?

Then help your child check people's answers against the Genesis 3 account. If your interviews are in person, you may want to document them with a camcorder or sound recorder and share them with the rest of the family later.

4. SPLASHDOWN:
Applying What You've Learned

What you need:
- *a Bible*
- *craft sticks*
- *marker*
- *modeling clay or dough*

Read Romans 3:23. Explain that we, like Adam and Eve, have disobeyed God. This is called sin, and it separates us from God just as the sin of Adam and Eve did.

Ask your child to name things that kids and moms and dads do wrong. Be as specific as possible. Here are suggestions to prompt your thinking:

- not sharing a toy or game
- talking back to parents instead of obeying
- sneaking more time to play video games by pretending to forget the time limit
- calling someone at school a name
- picking a fight with a sibling to get him in trouble
- being jealous of another family's bigger TV
- lying about whether you did a chore
- cheating on a test

As your child names each sin, write it on a separate craft stick (or draw a symbol, for pre-readers), push the stick into a bit of clay or

ALTERNATE FLIGHT PLAN:
Options for Ages 8-12

If you didn't make a Garden of Eden model and don't want to build a fence of craft sticks, here's another way to introduce the idea of being "shut out" by sin. Have your child write kinds of disobedience on strips of crepe paper and tape them over the entrance to his or her room. Announce, tongue in cheek, that he or she will be sleeping in the bathroom from now on. Discuss the kinds of lifestyle changes such an "exile" would require.

dough, and use the sticks to build a fence separating the figures from the Garden.

When you've built a sizable fence, talk a little about how our sins are like a wall between us and God. Ask how it feels to be shut out of a place your child would really like to be—a party, a theme park, a movie, a toy store.

Assure your child that God is just as eager as we are to knock down the fence and bring us close to Him. You'll be talking more about that in a future Family Time.

SPACE SNACK

What you need:
- *ice cream*
- *chocolate cookies or chocolate graham crackers*
- *sealable plastic bag*
- *gummy worms*
- *bowls*

Want to wrap up with refreshments? Try "garden sundaes." Give your child a bowl of ice cream. Let him or her crush chocolate cookies or chocolate graham crackers in a plastic bag and pour the resulting "dirt" on the ice cream. Add gummy worms as desired.

FAMILY TIME 7

PAYING THE PRICE

MISSION CONTROL:
Where You're Headed

You'll help your child understand that Jesus is God—and that He came in human form, lived a perfect life, and gave His life as payment for our sin.

COUNTDOWN:
Getting Ready

"It's not fair!" Chances are you've heard those words more than once from your child. Kids have a finely developed sense of justice—at least when they think they're the ones being treated unfairly!

In the *Adventures in Odyssey* episode you're about to listen to, your child will encounter the ultimate in unfairness: Jesus, the only perfect, sinless person who ever lived, is condemned to die the death of a criminal.

In a future Family Time you'll walk with your child down the "Romans Road" of receiving Christ, gaining a step-by-step understanding of how to benefit from His sacrifice. This time, though, you'll take a heart-level look at what it cost Jesus to bridge the gap our sin has created between us and God.

As you prepare to spend this time together, pray that your child's heart will be touched to respond to the unselfish love Jesus has for us. This Family Time may be an important step in readying your child to say yes to Him.

1. BLAST OFF:
Getting Started

What you need:
* *costumes and props (optional)*

If weather permits, enjoy this activity outdoors. If not, clear as much space as you can indoors and put breakables out of harm's way.

Play a game of cops and robbers or any other imaginative exercise that involves "good guys" and "bad guys." Give your child the

ALTERNATE FLIGHT PLAN:
Options for Ages 8-12

Let your older kids create the setting and characters for the role-playing. Foam rubber swords, water pistols, or plastic light sabers can make the game more appealing to pre-teens.

role of a "bad guy." Make sure he or she gets arrested and brought to "jail."

As sheriff, sternly explain the charges and punishment—10 years in jail, for instance, or whatever sentence you want to impose.

Before you carry out the sentence, however, spring a surprise on the prisoner. Announce that he or she is set free. Put another player—or yourself—in jail.

After calling an end to the role-playing, ask questions like these:

Do you think it was fair for one person to go free while an innocent person took the punishment?

If you were the person going free, how would you feel?

If you were the person being punished for something you didn't do, how would you feel?

Explain that you'll be listening to an *Adventures in Odyssey* episode. Invite your child to listen especially for whether Jesus was treated fairly, and how He responded.

 ## 2. EXPLORATION:
Discovering Truth

What you need:
- FaithLaunch *audio CD, tracks 4-6, "Imagination Station 1"*
- *CD player*
- *paper and markers*

Get comfortable and listen to the *Adventures in Odyssey* episode "Imagination Station 1." To help your child concentrate on the story, and to prepare for the wrap-up activity you'll be doing later, provide paper and markers; ask your child to draw pictures of the events.

3. REENTRY:
Bringing the Truth Home

At the conclusion of the episode, ask:

How is what happened in our game of "cops and robbers" a little like what happened to Jesus?

If you were the one being punished for something you didn't do, what would you say or do? What did Jesus say or do?

God says that people who disobey Him must be punished. Jesus never did anything wrong, but He took the punishment for our sins. Why would He do that? (Because He loves us.)

How does it make you feel to know that Jesus loves you enough to do that for you?

4. SPLASHDOWN:
Applying What You've Learned

What you need:
- *pictures your child drew while listening to the* Odyssey *episode*
- *paper, scissors, glue*

Have your child cut out one or more of the pictures he or she drew while listening to *Adventures in Odyssey*. Ask: **Let's say you're going to send a thank-you card to Jesus for what He's done for you. Using the art you drew, what kind of card can you make? What will your message to Jesus be?**

If your child can't write yet, help him or her put the card together. If your child has trouble coming up with a message, explain what you might write if it were your card. Let your child express his or her thoughts, however, rather than looking for a "right" answer.

If your child seems especially moved by the story or has questions about Jesus, take time to talk things over. If he or she wants to respond to the sacrifice of Jesus by praying to receive Him, you may want to suggest the prayer at the end of Family Time 10 (see page 89). Otherwise, simply encourage your child to put the card in a prominent place (his or her dresser, the refrigerator door, etc.) to remind him or her of what Jesus did.

ALTERNATE FLIGHT PLAN:
Options for Ages 8-12

What you need:
- *CD of worship songs*
- *CD player*

If your older child enjoys music, find a contemporary Christian CD that includes at least one song expressing gratitude to Jesus for His unselfish love. After listening to the song together, ask your child a few questions like these:

How do you feel after hearing that song?

If you had to pick one phrase from the song that sums it all up, what would it be?

How would you change that song to make it reflect your feelings more closely?

SPACE SNACK

What you need:
- *a dozen cookies, granola bars, strawberries, or other treats*
- *plates*

If you'd like to finish with refreshments, try this. Fill a plate with a dozen of anything your child likes to eat. Give yourself (and any other family members participating) a plate, too.

Let your child decide how to divide up the food. To get him or her thinking, ask: **What would be the "fairest" way to split this up? Based on the story we just heard, how do you think Jesus would do it? Why?**

FAMILY TIME 8

SURPRISE ENDING

MISSION CONTROL:
Where You're Headed

You'll help your child grasp the key events and meaning of Jesus' death and resurrection.

COUNTDOWN:
Getting Ready

Jesus' death and resurrection are the central events, not just of Christianity, but of all human history. With His sacrifice on the cross and His resurrection from the tomb, Jesus paid the death sentence for our sin. That's something to celebrate!

Try making this Family Time extra special for your child by dyeing Easter eggs—no matter what time of year it is. Fans of the Easter

Bunny may have claimed the Easter egg as their own, but you can use the symbolism of the egg (as described in the "Blast Off" step) so that every time your child sees a jelly bean, candy egg, or Easter egg, he or she will be reminded of the Savior who emerged alive from the grip of death.

You'll be listening to an *Adventures in Odyssey* episode, too—one that will help your child understand the events of the Easter season and how he or she can respond in faith.

1. BLAST OFF:
Getting Started

What you need:
- *boiled eggs*
- *Easter egg dyeing kit—or food coloring, distilled vinegar, water*
- *glass or metal cups or bowls*
- *stainless steel or disposable plastic spoons*
- *newspaper or waxed paper*
- *pan and stove*

No matter what time of year it is, celebrate Easter! Start this Family Time by dyeing Easter eggs with your child. If a dyeing kit isn't available, make your own coloring solution by mixing 2/3 cup of hot water with two teaspoons of distilled vinegar in a glass or metal cup or bowl; add food coloring a drop at a time until you have the desired hue. Let the mixture cool before using it. Put a stainless steel or disposable plastic spoon in each cup or bowl to maneuver your hard-boiled eggs.

As you work together, explain that, long ago, people were amazed to see something alive (a little chick) come out of something

ALTERNATE FLIGHT PLAN:
Options for Ages 8-12

What you'll need:
* *modeling clay or dough*
* *Bible or Bible picture encyclopedia*

Many older kids enjoy dyeing Easter eggs, too. But if you'd like a more "mature" activity, work together to make a model of Christ's empty tomb.

Research what the tomb might have looked like by reading Matthew 27:59-60 or by looking in a good Bible picture encyclopedia.

that looked like a stone (an egg). Eggs became a symbol for new life. The Easter egg can remind us of the stone cave where Jesus was buried—and from which He came out alive.

2. EXPLORATION:
Discovering Truth

What you need:
* FaithLaunch *audio CD, tracks 7-9, "Imagination Station 2"*
* *CD player*
* *modeling clay or dough (optional)*

Get comfortable and listen to the *Adventures in Odyssey* episode "Imagination Station 2." If you think it would help your child to concentrate on the story, provide a lump of modeling clay or dough and encourage him or her to sculpt some of the objects or people mentioned.

3. REENTRY:
Bringing the Truth Home

Prompt your child to talk about the episode by asking questions like the following, choosing those that are appropriate for your child's age and level of understanding.

The drama didn't explain exactly how Jesus died. What do you know about His death? (He was nailed to a wooden cross, a common way to put criminals to death in those days.)

If you'd been there when Jesus died, what do you think you would have done? How would you have felt?

What difference does it make that Jesus didn't stay dead, but came back to life? (It shows His power over death, and that we can trust God's promise of eternal life to those who believe in Jesus.)

The guard tells Barabbas, "You are free. Jesus has taken your place." In what way has Jesus taken *your* place? (He was punished for the wrong things we've done.)

How does it make you feel that Jesus suffered for you?

If Digger tells people about Jesus, what do you think he will say?

4. SPLASHDOWN:
Applying What You've Learned

What you need:
- *a Bible*
- *paper and pencil*

In the *Adventures in Odyssey* episode you just listened to, Jesus asks Digger, "Will you now also believe?"

Explain to your child how you'd answer that question. Share a

little about the joy your faith brings you, and how living for Jesus is
the best adventure ever.

Then ask, **How about you? Do you believe in Jesus?**

If your child says yes, ask, **What are some things you believe
about Him?** After listening to your child's answer, affirm as much of
it as you can. Clear up misconceptions your child might have about
Jesus or about the process of beginning a relationship with God. If
you need more information, don't panic; promise to look for what
you need during the next few days. You may find it helpful to check
the questions and answers in Part III of this book.

If your child is ready to express belief in Jesus through prayer,
you may want to lead him or her in the prayer found at the end of
Family Time 10 (see page 89).

If your child says no—that he or she doesn't believe—ask
whether you can answer any questions about Jesus. Plan to find and

SPACE SNACK

What you need:

• *Easter-themed goodies*

If it happens to be Easter time, you've got it made—
just buy your family's favorite chocolate bunnies, marshmallow chicks, or candy eggs. During the rest of the
year, though, you'll need to be a little more creative.
Jelly beans, yogurt-covered raisins, or chocolate-coated
peanuts can stand in for eggs.

Prefer a snack with more protein than sugar? Serve
the hard-boiled eggs you just decorated!

share answers before your next Family Time. If your child doesn't believe and doesn't have questions, avoid pressing him or her to respond more positively. Keep praying for your child and look for opportunities to be an example of Jesus' love for him or her.

If your child has already prayed to receive Jesus, remind him or her that in the story you listened to, Digger wanted to tell people about Jesus. Read aloud the Bible passage that Mr. Whittaker refers to at the end of the episode, Matthew 28:18-20. Together, make a list of people your child could tell about Jesus. Pray for each of them.

FAMILY TIME 9

A BRAND-NEW FATHER

MISSION CONTROL:
Where You're Headed

You'll help your child see that God wants us to be part of His family—and that because of Jesus, we can.

COUNTDOWN:
Getting Ready

Everything you've been sharing with your child—that Christ took the consequences for our sins, the powerful truth of His resurrection—points to the amazing fact that God wants a relationship with us. He wants us to be His children.

Launching your child's faith isn't just about knowing facts or praying prayers. It's about starting an eternal, personal bond with our Creator through His Son. Your child needs to know that salvation isn't a coldhearted legal transaction. It's an adoption motivated by love stronger than we can imagine.

1. BLAST OFF:
Getting Started

What you need:
- *treasure-hunt clues on sticky notes (see below)*
- *a picture of yourself*
- *small prize*

Before Family Time, set up a "treasure hunt" with clues for your child to follow. On each clue, include not only the hint or directions to the next clue, but also a brief note telling your child how much you love him or her.

If you can tie the love note into the location, that's even better! For example, "I love reading with you. Go to our favorite reading spot," could lead to the chair you sit in together when you read to your child.

Have the last clue lead to the "treasure": a picture of you.

Follow your child during the treasure hunt, so you can help with any tricky clues and enjoy the fun together. Pick up the clues as you go and carry them with you.

ALTERNATE FLIGHT PLAN:
Options for Ages 8-12

Most older kids like treasure hunts, too. To keep it fun for your older child, make the clues more challenging. Include rhyming or visual clues—even math problems.

Here's an example: "You'll find the next clue in a 3.14159265 pan." The answer: "Pi (pie) pan."

When you reach the treasure, ask: **What do you think of this treasure?**

Chances are your child will be a little disappointed—especially if he or she was expecting candy or money. Reach into your pocket and produce another treasure—a prize like a dollar bill.

Ask: **What do you think of *this* treasure?**

Your child may be more enthused about the prize than about your picture. Say: **This picture stands for me. If you didn't have this treasure** [point to yourself] **would you have this one** [hold up the prize]?

Give your child the prize. Explain that there are two kinds of treasures—the people who love us, and the things those people give us *because* they love us. We need to remember not just the things, but the people, too.

2. EXPLORATION:
Discovering Truth

What you need:
- *Bible*
- *the clues from your treasure hunt*
- *sticky note*
- *pen or pencil*

Show your child the notes from the treasure hunt. Ask: **Why do you think I wrote these to you?**

Your child may give any number of responses; here are some possibilities, along with ways to tie them into the truth that God wants to have a relationship with us.

- "You wrote the notes and clues because you're my mommy/daddy."

That's right! I'm your mommy [or daddy], **and I love you! So I wrote you notes to tell you that I love you. God is your heavenly**

Father, and He loves you, too. Did you know that He wrote you notes to tell you He loves you? They're in the Bible.

• "You wrote the notes and clues so I could find the treasure."

Yes! I wanted you to find the treasure because I love you. God loves you, too, and He has an even better treasure for you—eternal life with Jesus. He wrote to you in the Bible to tell you how you can have that treasure.

• "You wrote the notes and clues because you like to read with me [or whatever you might have written in a note]."

I do like to read with you! I like being with you. God likes being with you, too. He even wants us to come live with Him forever someday.

Open the Bible to 1 John 3:1a and read it aloud. Here it is in the New International Version: "How great is the love the Father has lavished on us, that we should be called children of God! And that is what we are!"

God wants us to be part of His family! Because of Jesus, we can be God's children.

ALTERNATE FLIGHT PLAN:
Options for Ages 8-12

Use the word "relationship" with older kids. Ask them what kind of relationship they like to have with a friend, with you, and with a sibling. What kind of relationship would they like to have with God?

Help them understand the kind of relationship God would like to have with them by looking at John 14:23-27 and John 15:14-16. Then ask them to summarize the verses on a sticky note or two.

Ask: **Do you know what Jesus did that made it possible to be God's children?** After your child responds, confirm or clarify his or her answer by reading 1 John 2:12: **"Dear children, I'm writing to you because your sins have been forgiven. They have been forgiven because of what Jesus has done"** (NIrV).

Explain that this is one of God's "notes" to you and your child, and it's worth remembering. Then help your child write or draw a summary of the verse on a sticky note.

3. REENTRY:
Bringing the Truth Home

What you need:
• *the sticky notes from your treasure hunt*

Collect the "love note" clues from your treasure hunt. Let your child decide where to put them (on his or her bedroom door, the bathroom mirror, etc.) as a reminder that you and God love your child. The only rule: No more than three notes may be posted in any one room. That should help ensure that your child encounters the messages as often as possible.

4. SPLASHDOWN:
Applying What You've Learned

What you need:
• *ice cubes*
• *mitten or glove*

Give your child an ice cube; see how long he or she can hold it before wanting to get rid of it because it's cold or messy. Then let your child wear a mitten or glove to warm up his or her hand.

Ask: **Which does God want to be like to you—an ice cube that's cold and hard, or a mitten that's warm and protects you?**

As needed, point out that God wants to be warm, close, and loving to the members of His family. That's why He invites us to join His family by believing in His Son, Jesus.

If your child hasn't responded to that invitation yet, ask whether he or she would like to do so now. If the answer is yes, you may want to lead your child in the prayer found at the end of Family Time 10.

If the answer is no, don't press. You may want to pray with your child, though, asking God to help him or her to discover the treasure of getting to know the One who loves us so much. The next Family Time will explain more thoroughly how to do that, and will provide another opportunity to respond.

SPACE SNACK

What you need:
- *a "treasure" snack (see below)*

In keeping with the "treasure" theme, you may want to try one of the following treats:

- foil-wrapped chocolate coins
- any food with the word "Gold" or "Jewel" in its name
- any candy resembling a jewel, necklace, or gold nugget
- any food that hides one ingredient inside another (celery sticks filled with peanut butter or cheese, cream-filled snack cakes, etc.)

FAMILY TIME 10

THE ROMANS ROAD

MISSION CONTROL:
Where You're Headed

You'll help your child understand the steps he or she can take to begin a relationship with God.

COUNTDOWN:
Getting Ready

If you could choose just one message from the Bible to share with your child, wouldn't it be the Good News of how to be right with God?

Perhaps your child already has a relationship with God. Then this Family Time will be a happy reminder of God's grace in your lives, and maybe a model of how to share the Good News with others.

If your child hasn't received Jesus as Savior and Lord, this Family Time provides an opportunity to do so. It's your privilege to point the way and invite your child to "believe in his heart and confess with his mouth" that Jesus is Lord.

Pave the way with prayer. It's both humbling and reassuring to know that any "results" will be God's doing, not yours. If you don't see results, don't panic. God may build on this Family Time according to His schedule—and in ways you can't predict.

1. BLAST OFF:
Getting Started

What you need:
- *two tables or cardboard cartons*
- *paper plates*
- *bag of marshmallows*
- *building blocks*
- *toy car*
- *prize (optional)*

Set up two tables or cardboard cartons with a gap of about three feet between them. Supply one or more toy cars.

Issue a challenge to everyone in the family: **We're about to become bridge builders. Your job is to build a bridge that will carry this toy car from one table [or box] to the other. But you can only use the materials I'm about to show you.**

Bring out a stack of paper plates, a bag of marshmallows, and a set of building blocks. Working alone or in teams, family members have five minutes to come up with bridges that support the car.

When time is up, let people demonstrate their bridges. Anyone whose bridge works gets to eat a leftover marshmallow—or is awarded a prize of your choice.

ALTERNATE FLIGHT PLAN:
Options for Ages 8-12

What you need:
• *paper*

Older kids may enjoy the extra challenge of using only paper to make their bridges (and if your kids aren't younger, you might not have a set of building blocks around anymore).

Don't let participants use tape or staples; they can't use scissors to cut the paper either, but can only tear. Folding the paper for added strength is allowed, as is connecting pieces of paper by tearing tabs that fit into slots.

Ask: **How well did your bridge work? Why? What would have made this project easier?**

Have you ever wished you could get from one side of something—like a puddle, a canyon, or a river—to the other? When you can't jump far enough, what do you need? (A bridge, an airplane, somebody to carry you, etc.)

Explain that there's a space everybody needs to get across—and nobody can do it alone. We need a bridge, and there's only one that works.

2. EXPLORATION:
Discovering Truth

What you need:
• *a Bible*
• *paper*
• *pencils*

Tell your child that you're going to draw a different kind of bridge. It's on the "Romans Road," based on the Book of Romans in the Bible.

Read aloud Romans 3:10-12 and Romans 3:23. Draw a diagram like the following on your paper. Have your child copy your drawing on his or her own sheet. Encourage your child to draw a picture of himself or herself on the "People" side of the diagram.

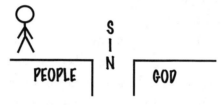

Next read Romans 6:23. Say something like, **All of us have sinned—done things that are wrong. What's the "pay" for sin?** (Death)

What does God offer to give you instead? (Life)

[Note: Very young children may not understand the nature or permanence of death. If this is the case with your child, you may want to emphasize instead the idea of being apart from God, who loves us. The concept of separation is made clear in the "Romans Road" diagram.]

If your child understands what death is, add the words "Death" and "Life" as shown in the following illustration—and have your child do the same. For younger children, drawing sad and happy faces in place of "Death" and "Life" may be more effective.

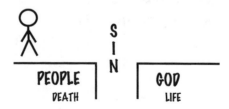

Now read Romans 5:8. Add the rest of the cross to your drawing as shown. If your child can read, write in the name of Christ. Encourage your child to do the same.

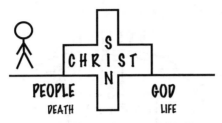

ALTERNATE FLIGHT PLAN:
Options for Ages 8-12

With older kids, your discussion of the life Christ offers can go into more detail. As you read the following passages, you might explore them with questions like these.

Romans 3:10-12: **What kind of a life does this describe? Is yours ever like this? Is it the life you want?**

Romans 5:8: **What does this tell you about God? Why do people call this the Good News?**

Romans 10:9-10: **Does this describe you? Which part sounds harder—believing or telling others that you believe?**

Romans 10:13: **Does it sound too easy to get started in a relationship with God? How did God actually get things started? Would you say His part was easy or hard?**

Read Romans 10:9-10. Explain that to cross the bridge to God, all you need to do is ask Him to forgive your sins, believe in Jesus as your rescuer, and say so. Draw in the line that indicates crossing the bridge, as in the following diagram.

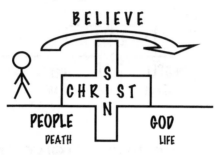

3. REENTRY:
Bringing the Truth Home

What you need:
• *Bible*
• *the "Romans Road" your child drew*

To be sure your child understands, invite him or her to describe the Romans Road to you by using the diagram he or she drew. Afterward, place the diagram in this book; you'll be using it again in your next Family Time.

4. SPLASHDOWN:
Applying What You've Learned

What you need:
• *Bible*

Read Romans 10:13. Make sure your child understands the promise: God will save, or rescue, anyone who asks.

If your child has already asked, celebrate that together. Affirm that God will keep His Romans 10:13 promise.

If your child hasn't asked, provide the opportunity to do so. Invite him or her to offer a prayer along the following lines.

Dear God,

I know that without You I'm messed up. I know that I sin—I do things that are wrong and don't do things I should. You said You love me even though I'm still a sinner. Will You please forgive me and give me a new start?

I want You to be my heavenly Father. I believe Your Son, Jesus, died to pay the price for my sin and rose to life again. I accept Him as my Savior to rescue me, and as my Lord to be in charge of my life.

In Jesus' name I pray. Amen.

If your child isn't ready to pray a prayer like that, ask which parts of the prayer he or she isn't sure about. This may give you some clues about concepts to review as you complete the remaining three *Faith-Launch* Family Times.

SPACE SNACK

What you need:
- *refreshments of your choice*
- *your best dishes*

If you're celebrating your child's decision to receive Christ, whether that happened long ago or just now, the food may not matter as much as the way in which it's served. Try marking the occasion by bringing out your best dishes—even if the fare is potato chips and fruit punch.

FAMILY TIME 11

HOME
FREE

MISSION CONTROL:
Where You're Headed

You'll help your child discover that Jesus is preparing a place for us so that we can spend eternity with Him.

COUNTDOWN:
Getting Ready

Nothing gives a child security like a happy home. In this Family Time, you have the privilege of introducing your child to the security of our eternal home with Jesus.

We don't know all the details of what that home will be like—though it may be fun and revealing to get your child's ideas about it. But we do know the most important thing: Those who belong to Jesus will be with Him forever. That's true security.

1. BLAST OFF:
Getting Started

What you need:

• *your child's baby book, photos, or video*

Curl up with your child and look together at his or her baby book (or DVD, or whatever format in which you've stored photos or video). As you look at the pictures, emphasize the preparations you made in your home to welcome your child. For example, you might say something like the following.

Here's a picture of you in your crib. Before you were born [or adopted], I picked out a special, soft blanket to keep you all cozy in your crib. Look—you can see your wallpaper in this picture. Did you know that when Daddy and I were putting it on the wall, we almost pasted it upside down?

Tell your child how excited you were to be expecting him or her, how much you enjoyed preparing, and how eager you were for the

ALTERNATE FLIGHT PLAN:
Options for Ages 8-12

Younger children aren't the only ones who like being reminded of how special their arrival was. Most older kids do, too—though the "curling up" and "Mommy and Daddy" references may not apply.

Your older child may also have experience preparing a place for a new pet, a train set, a computer, or a basketball hoop. If so, invite your child to recall his or her preparations and anticipation.

day when you could bring him or her home from the hospital or adoption agency.

Then ask: **When you were a baby, what do you think you liked better—cuddling in your baby blanket, or cuddling in Mommy's or Daddy's arms?** That's right! You liked being with Mommy and Daddy better.

When you were a baby, what do you think you liked better—looking at your mobile [or wallpaper, or whatever applies], or looking at Mommy's or Daddy's face? That's right! You liked looking at Mommy and Daddy better.

When you were a baby, what do you think you liked better—playing with your rattle, or playing with Mommy or Daddy? That's right! You liked playing with Mommy and Daddy better.

You liked all the special things in the room we prepared for you. But what made you happiest was being with Mommy and Daddy, because we loved you so much!

 ## 2. EXPLORATION:
Discovering Truth

What you need:
• *Bible*

Read aloud John 14:2-4. Make sure your child understands that Jesus is talking in these verses.

Say something like this:

We prepared a place for you when you joined our family. Who prepares a place for you when you join God's family? (Jesus)

I wonder what it'll be like to live in God's house. What do you think? Enjoy wondering together with your child. None of us really

ALTERNATE FLIGHT PLAN:
Options for Ages 8-12

Older kids can make their own connection between your preparation for them as babies and Jesus' preparations in John 14:2-4. Instead of making the comparison yourself, try asking questions like the following.

How is this Bible passage like what we did when you became part of our family?

What do you think the place that Jesus is preparing will be like?

What do you think will be the best thing about living with Jesus? Why?

knows what to expect, so don't worry about leading your child to the "right" answers.

When you were a baby, you liked the place we prepared for you. But what made you happiest was being with us, because we loved you so much! When you get to live with Jesus, what do you think will be best—the things He's prepared for you, or being with God, because He loves you so much?

3. REENTRY:
Bringing the Truth Home

What you need:

• *magazines and newspapers*

Point out that the place Jesus is preparing for us is perfect—a place full of joy, without sickness or war or death. Bring out a stack of magazines and newspapers, preferably ones that feature plenty of pictures. Say something like: **We'll see some amazing things in** heaven. But there are also some things we won't see. Can you think of any? Can you find pictures of any of them in these newspapers and magazines?

Look together for pictures of things you're unlikely to see in heaven. Here are some examples:

- Hospitals, ambulances, medicine
- Cemeteries, funerals
- Crime scenes, fights, police cars, battlefields, jails
- Car accidents, burning buildings
- Floods, tornadoes, famines, other disasters

Read Revelation 21:3-4. Ask: **How do you feel when you hear about this place? How does it feel to know that Jesus is getting it ready for us?**

 ## 4. SPLASHDOWN:
Applying What You've Learned

What you need:
- *Bible*
- *the "Romans Road" diagram your child drew in Family Time 10*

Read John 14:2-4 again. **What does Jesus mean when He says we know the way to the place where He's going? How do we get there?**

Show your child the diagram of the Romans Road that he or she drew. Remind him or her how it shows the way to living forever with Jesus in the home He prepares for us.

As needed, use the picture to talk through the process as you did in Family Time 10. Reaffirm that you and your child will be able to live with Jesus forever because of what Jesus did on the cross. If your child hasn't prayed to receive Jesus as Savior and Lord, invite him or her to do so.

SPACE SNACK

What you need:
- *"banquet" foods (see below)*
- *tea party set (optional)*

Revelation 19:9 mentions the "wedding supper of the Lamb" in heaven. You and your child can start celebrating now with a scaled-down "banquet" of your own. For younger children, a tea party with miniature plates and cups might be in order; older kids may prefer a smorgasbord of fruit, popcorn, cheese, or other snacks.

FAMILY TIME 12

FOLLOWING THE LEADER

MISSION CONTROL:
Where You're Headed

You'll help your child discover that Jesus taught us how to pray and how to live.

COUNTDOWN:
Getting Ready

If your child has decided to begin a relationship with God, that's great. But praying to receive Jesus as Savior and Lord is the start of the launch, not the end. It's like "Ignition!" in a rocket's takeoff; the next step is to get moving.

Your child needs to know that following Jesus is about faith *and* action. The Lord's Prayer is a good place to start.

When Jesus' disciples asked Him to teach them how to pray, He responded with the words that have become known as the Lord's Prayer. In it Jesus teaches us not only how to pray, but how to live— as those who keep God's name holy, who work for the coming of His kingdom, and who follow His will.

Whether the Lord's Prayer is new or familiar to your child, you can use it to show him or her that in God's family we try to live out what we pray for. Even if your child hasn't prayed that "Ignition!" prayer yet, this Family Time can give him or her a more complete picture of what a relationship with God is all about.

1. BLAST OFF:
Getting Started

As a family, play a game of "Mother, May I?"

"Mother" (who can just as easily be played by a father) stands at one end of the room. Everyone else stands at the other. Each player (other than "Mother") takes a turn asking for permission to move forward in a specific number of baby steps, giant steps, or bunny hops.

Mother answers, "Yes," or, "No, but you may take [number] baby steps [or giant steps, or bunny hops]."

This instruction isn't enough, however, to allow the player to move. The player must still get permission by asking, "Mother, may I?"

If Mother says, "Yes, you may," the player moves. If Mother says, "No, you may not," the player stays put. A player who forgets to ask permission returns to the starting line.

After a round or two played this way, tell players that for the rest of the game they may ask only for bunny hops or baby steps, not giant steps. Whenever a player asks for bunny hops or baby steps, say, "Yes." Requests for giant steps get an automatic "No."

When you're done playing, say something like the following.

When you asked for the things I wanted you to ask for, I

always said "Yes," didn't I? I taught you what to ask for, and that taught you what to do.

When Jesus gave us the Lord's Prayer, He taught us what to ask God for. That teaches us what to do when we're part of God's family.

ALTERNATE FLIGHT PLAN:
Options for Ages 8-12

What you need:
• *a prize (optional)*

Are your kids too old for "Mother, May I?" Send them on a scavenger hunt to find things that represent ways to communicate.

For example, a phone book could symbolize telephoning; a cell phone could stand for text messaging; stationery or postage stamps could represent writing a letter; a computer keyboard could symbolize e-mail or instant messaging; a Bible could represent books; a camcorder could stand for videoconferencing; an MP3 player could represent podcasting; a microphone could stand for plain old conversation. Set a time limit of five minutes and see who can gather the most symbols. If you like, award a prize to the winner.

Then ask: **What could you use to represent prayer?** (Perhaps the "praying hands" symbol, or your knees, or a length of chain [as in "prayer chain"].)

Note that when Jesus gave us the Lord's Prayer, He taught us not only how to communicate with God, but also how to live in ways that please God.

2. EXPLORATION:
Discovering Truth

What you need:
- *Bible*
- *three sheets of paper*
- *crayons or markers*
- *stapler*

Put three sheets of paper together and fold them in half to create a blank 5 1/2" x 8" book. Staple along the fold so the pages stay together.

Help your child turn the pages into a picture book about the Lord's Prayer. First, write "The Lord's Prayer" on the cover. Then write one phrase of the prayer on each page inside the booklet, copying from Matthew 6:9-13. If your church uses the following conclusion, add that, too: "For Yours is the kingdom, and the power, and the glory forever. Amen."

ALTERNATE FLIGHT PLAN:
Options for Ages 8-12

Unless your older child is a budding author or illustrator, he or she might not get excited about creating a picture book. Keep the "Lord's Prayer" idea, but try one of these alternatives and show it to the rest of the family:

- Make a PowerPoint slide show using graphics found online.
- Use a camcorder to make a video.
- Make a slide show using a digital camera.

If your child isn't old enough to write without frustration, do the writing for him or her.

Next, team up to illustrate each page. Use this time to talk about what each part of the prayer means. Here are some explanations you might use:

- *Our Father in heaven.* (We can come to You because we're part of Your family.)
- *Hallowed be Your name.* (May people keep Your name holy, treating it specially because of who You are.)
- *Your kingdom come.* (We want You to be the Ruler everywhere.)
- *Your will be done on earth as it is in heaven.* (May people obey You completely.)
- *Give us today our daily bread.* (Please meet our needs for food and other things.)
- *Forgive us our debts.* (Please forgive us for disobeying You.)
- *As we forgive our debtors.* (We forgive those who've wronged us.)
- *And lead us not into temptation.* (Please help us not to disobey You.)
- *But deliver us from the evil one.* (Protect us from the devil's plans.)
- *For Yours is the kingdom, and the power, and the glory forever. Amen.* (You're the rightful Ruler of everything and everyone. That's right!)

3. REENTRY:
Bringing the Truth Home

What you need:
- *the book you and your child made*

To help your child remember the Lord's Prayer, use the book you made. Read it aloud a page at a time, leaving out one of the key

ALTERNATE FLIGHT PLAN:
Options for Ages 8-12

What you need:
- *index cards*
- *marker*

If your older child hasn't memorized the Lord's Prayer, here's a fun way to do it. Work together to write the prayer on index cards, one word per card. Collect the cards, shuffle them thoroughly, and dump them on the floor or table. See how quickly your child can arrange them in order.

Then reshuffle the cards and see whether you can beat your child's time. If possible, try one more round apiece to help set the wording of the prayer in your child's mind.

words on the page. For example: "_____ be Your name." See whether your child can call out the missing word.

If your child can read, let him or her test your memory in the same way.

4. SPLASHDOWN:
Applying What You've Learned

To help your child connect the Lord's Prayer to everyday actions, use questions like the following—adapting them as needed to fit your child's age and experience with biblical concepts.

How can you show respect for God's name? Is that harder to do in some places than in others?

What do you think it means for God's kingdom to come? How can our family help that to happen?

What's one thing you think God wants you to do? If you *didn't* want God's will to be done in that area, what would your actions be like?

How hard is it to be thankful for your "daily bread" when we have _____ [name a food your child dislikes] for supper? What do you think God wants you to do then?

Is there anybody you're mad at right now? What if God forgave you exactly as much as you've forgiven that person?

What temptation do you especially need God's help to resist tomorrow?

If your child is comfortable with the idea, consider letting him or her lead your family in saying the Lord's Prayer at the dinner table one night this week.

ALTERNATE FLIGHT PLAN:
Options for Ages 8-12

Challenge older kids to pick one part of the Lord's Prayer that they especially need to work on this week. Use their answers to the questions in the "Splashdown" section to help them choose.

For example, if they hinted that taking God's name in vain is a temptation, they could focus on "Hallowed be Your name." Or if complaining about a particular food is a problem, they could concentrate on being more grateful for what God provides.

SPACE SNACK

What you need:
- *"daily bread" snack (see below)*

If you'd like to reflect the "daily bread" portion of the Lord's Prayer, try serving one of the following:

- flour tortillas with honey or salsa
- biscuits and jam
- breadsticks with cinnamon and sugar
- rolls and melted cheese to dip them in

WHAT LOVE LOOKS LIKE

MISSION CONTROL:
Where You're Headed

You'll help your child understand and apply the truth that God wants us to love others.

COUNTDOWN:
Getting Ready

You've been guiding your child to know and love God. But the writer of 1 John tells us that if we don't love other people, we don't really love God (1 John 4:20). This is a good time to let your child know that having a relationship with God means, among other things, loving one's neighbor.

Talk about a practical commandment! Your child can see what "love your neighbor" looks like. Sharing with friends. Obeying parents.

Getting along with brothers and sisters—even when it's "not fair."

If you want an instruction your child can practice right away as he or she leaves the launchpad of faith, this is it! The same is true if you want a quality *you* can model daily. The best way to teach it is by word and example.

1. BLAST OFF:
Getting Started

What you need:
- *Bible*
- *stuffed animals, dolls, action figures*
- *costumes (optional)*
- *video camera (optional)*

Explain that you're going to read a Bible story and that your child and the rest of the family get to act it out. Assign family members (and stuffed animals, dolls, or action figures) to the following parts:

- traveler
- robber
- priest
- Levite
- Good Samaritan
- donkey (optional)
- innkeeper (optional)

Read the story of the Good Samaritan from Luke 10:30-37 in an easy-to-understand version as family members pantomime (and manipulate the stuffed animals, dolls, or action figures).

If you have a video camera, you might record the "performance." Then view it while you discuss the questions in the next section.

2. EXPLORATION:
Discovering Truth

What you need:
- *Bible*
- *the characters (family members and toys) from the "Blast Off" section*

Explain that Jesus told the story of the Good Samaritan to show how we should act toward other people. Point to the person (or toy) who represented the robber and ask, **Is this the way Jesus wants us to treat others?**

Repeat with the characters representing the priest, the Levite, and the Good Samaritan.

Then ask: **Why treat people the way Jesus wants us to? Why not just do whatever we feel like doing?**

As needed, point out that part of being in God's family means following Jesus. Read what He said in John 14:15: **"If you love me, you will obey what I command."**

ALTERNATE FLIGHT PLAN:
Options for Ages 8-12

Older kids can grasp that we're fakes if we claim to love God but don't love others. Ask your child to read 1 John 4:20: "If anyone says, 'I love God,' yet hates his brother, he is a liar. For anyone who does not love his brother, whom he has seen, cannot love God, whom he has not seen."

Ask: **Which of the people in the Good Samaritan story probably would have said they loved God? Would you have believed them? Why or why not?**

3. REENTRY:
Bringing the Truth Home

Challenge your child to come up with a just-for-fun secret code—a language that only he or she understands. It can use real or made-up words, weird noises, or even taps on a table. Then ask your child to "say" the following messages in this new code:

- "I'm hungry."
- "Jack and Jill went up the hill to fetch a pail of water."
- "I love you."

Have your child teach you how to say "I love you" in the code. Then say something like, **That's a strange way to tell me you love me! And I can think of some other strange ways to say that. I'm going to read a list of things a person might do. If you think an action would show love, give me a "thumbs up." If you think it wouldn't, give me a "thumbs down."**

- Stealing somebody's sandwich out of the refrigerator.

ALTERNATE FLIGHT PLAN:
Options for Ages 8-12

What you need:
- *paper*
- *pencil*

Your older child might like the added challenge of coming up with a secret code that can actually be used for two-way conversation. Have him or her write the letters of the alphabet on a piece of paper and assign a symbol or different letter to each. Your child can use this code to write the messages you read, including "I love you."

- Laughing at another kid's haircut.
- Painting a mustache on a girl's favorite doll.
- Ignoring a boy who just slipped and fell on an icy sidewalk.

Then say something like: **How do you know these things wouldn't be a good way to say, "I love you"?** (They'd hurt the other person; I wouldn't want someone to do them to me; Jesus wouldn't do them.)

4. SPLASHDOWN:
Applying What You've Learned

What you need:
- *stuffed animals, dolls, or action figures*

Reassemble the cast of toys you used to help you act out the Good Samaritan story. Ask your child to use the figures to show how

ALTERNATE FLIGHT PLAN:
Options for Ages 8-12

If your older child isn't enthused about role playing with toys, ask him or her to "direct" the two of you (or other family members if available) in scenarios like the following, showing what Jesus would and wouldn't have us do.

- Your brother is supposed to feed the cat, but isn't feeling well.
- Your sister forgot some of her lines in the play at church, and is so embarrassed she's locked herself in her room.
- A new student is being pushed around by a gang member behind the school.

Jesus would *not* want us to act—and then to demonstrate how Jesus *would* want us to act—in scenarios like the following.

- Two children want the same beach ball.
- Mom asks a child to set the table.
- A younger brother wants to play with you when you have a friend over.

To wrap up this final *FaithLaunch* Family Time, make sure your child understands that we love others because God loved us first (1 John 4:19)—not because we're trying to get God to love us. Loving others doesn't get us into God's family; eternal life with Him is a free gift to those who believe in Jesus.

If your child hasn't expressed that belief yet, this would be a good time to provide another opportunity. If your child doesn't want to place his or her faith in Jesus, be patient and keep praying; trust that he or she will respond to God's prompting in the future.

Regardless of your child's response, keep including a spiritual dimension in the times you spend together as a family. Whether through scheduled family events or impromptu teachable moments, continue to assure your child of your love, God's love, and the adventure that awaits everyone who accepts His invitation to join His family.

SPACE SNACK

What you need:
* *ingredients for two dozen brownies or cookies*
* *decorative tin*

You can enjoy refreshments—and show love to someone else. Using a mix to save time, let your child help you make two dozen brownies or cookies. Divide the finished batch in half. Put half the treats in a decorative tin; take this to someone in your neighborhood who you know would enjoy the gift. If possible, let your child make the presentation.

When you get home, have some of the remaining treats with your family.

PART III

HANDLING YOUR CHILD'S FAITH QUESTIONS[1]

As surely as splashdown follows liftoff, questions are bound to arise as you help launch your child's faith:

- "Why didn't God just forgive everybody instead of sending His Son to die for us?"
- "If God is so powerful, why didn't He answer my prayer to heal Grandpa?"
- "Now that I know Jesus, how am I supposed to follow Him?"

The rest of this book is devoted to helping you answer those questions. You'll find things to *tell* your child, and things to *do* that help illustrate your words. Some replies and activities are designed for younger children, some for older kids. Since you know your child best, you'll know which ones to choose—and which to adapt.

For even more answers, try the following resources:

- *801 Questions Kids Ask about God* by Dr. Bruce B. Barton, Jonathan Farrar, James C. Galvin, Daryl J. Lucas, Rick Osborne, David R. Veerman, and Dr. James Wilhoit (Tyndale House Publishers/Focus on the Family, 2000), for use with younger children;
- *Stand* by Alex McFarland (Focus on the Family/Tyndale House Publishers, 2005), for older kids and teens.

TOPIC 1

GOD

Q: How Do We Know God Is Real?

Is God really there? The apostle Paul pointed out that the world God created makes it obvious He exists. You can help your children understand that our beautiful, incredibly complicated, amazingly intertwined universe clearly shows the hand of a Creator.

"What may be known about God is plain to them, because God made it plain to them. For since the creation of the world God's invisible qualities—his eternal power and divine nature—have been clearly seen, being understood from what has been made, so that men are without excuse" (Romans 1:19-20).

Start with the assumption that your children already think God is real. Build on their belief. When they ask questions, assume they ask out of curiosity and a desire to know rather than out of skepticism. They want to have their faith bolstered. Make these truths a matter-of-fact, comforting addition to their faith.

Give your children good reasons to believe. Share with them the following aspects of creation, including some things found in ourselves, that show God's hand:

1. *Orderliness.* Things fall down, never up. Water boils when you add heat. Wood burns. Every day the sun rises and sets. The world is so predictable and orderly that scientists can make rules about it. This could not happen by chance. It makes sense to believe that God designed it all!

2. *Beauty.* From newborns to nasturtiums, the world is full of

beauty. Why? There's no reason for beauty except to give pleasure. Why "evolve" something with no function? Only God would make something purely for enjoyment.

3. *The God idea.* As long as there have been people, they have believed in God or gods. Where did that idea come from? God put it into people. He made humans to know that He's real. Even people who say they don't believe in God often turn to Him in trouble. We're made to need something or Someone other than ourselves—God.

4. *Right and wrong.* Listen to people argue and you'll hear, "But you promised!" "It's not fair." People think promises should be kept, and that fairness is important. How does everyone know this? Because there's a law or rule built into everyone that says so. Your conscience tells you when you break this "rule." Where did this law come from? From God, who made right and wrong—and people.

Q: What's God Like?

God made people in His image (Genesis 1:26-27), so your children are like Him in some ways. You can tell your kids that, like them, He feels emotions like sadness, anger, and joy; He also laughs, talks, thinks, makes things, and forms friendships. Knowing their "likeness to God" is important to children because it lets them know that God understands them and can help them. It also makes God more real to them—easier to believe in, relate to, and talk with (Hebrews 2:14, 18).

Here are some ways to make those points with your children:

• Have a family talent show. Let each child demonstrate an ability—anything from playing the piano to making funny faces. Afterward, talk about God's "talents." Which ones has He "passed on" to humans? Which ones has He reserved for Himself?

• During an upcoming meal, make God your guest. You may even want to set a place for Him as a reminder to your children that He's always there. As you laugh together, thank God for fun. When you mention how proud you are of your children, tell them God is, too. When they tell jokes, remind them that God has a sense of humor as well.

• Take your children out one at a time for lunch, dinner, miniature golf, or another activity. As you talk and listen, affirm your interest in your children's lives. Then let them know that God enjoys them, too. Remind them that God is thinking about them and likes being with them.

Though we're made in God's image, we certainly aren't His equals. Let your children know that, unlike us, God can do anything, knows everything, and is everywhere. Nothing is too hard for Him to do or too small for Him to bother with; there is nothing He doesn't understand; no place is out of His reach (Jeremiah 23:24; 32:17; Matthew 10:30; Matthew 19:26; Psalm 147:5). Understanding these truths will help your children trust God when the world seems scary, confusing, or out of control.

To help your kids understand those concepts, try the following:

• Young children are beginning to discover the vastness of God's creation. They often develop an interest in the solar system, volcanoes, dinosaurs, the undersea world, and other big things God has made. Check out library books and videos that describe the awesome size of Jupiter, the mind-boggling distances between stars, the depth of the seas. Look together at maps and globes that show how large countries and continents are. As you do, talk about how powerful God must be to make such gigantic things.

• Assure your children that they can ask God for big things. He can handle anything. Hinting that there are some requests they shouldn't make sows doubt and undermines trust. *But what if my kids want it to snow in the middle of summer?* you might wonder. Let them ask! They need to learn to go to God for everything—and trust Him to do what's best. Explain that sometimes this means His answer will be no—just as sometimes you, too, say no because a thing's not good for them, because the time isn't right, or because you have a better plan.

God is—among other things—true and honest, loving and compassionate, generous and selfless, forgiving and merciful, trustworthy and faithful, just and impartial, and holy. To help children remember God's character traits, use activities like the following:

• Encourage them to come up with a visual symbol for each trait; for example, a judge's gavel for justice and impartiality, and a bar of soap for holiness (purity). Have them draw these on a poster. Or use them in a guessing game, to see whether family members can figure out what the symbols represent.

• As you teach your children what God is like, help them to see small ways in which they can develop some of the same character traits. For instance, a child might reflect God's generosity by letting a sibling read a favorite magazine first when it comes in the mail. Encourage children to commit to a specific action to be carried out on a specific day.

Q: Is There One God, or Three?

There's only one God (Isaiah 43:10; 44:6). Hearing this can be welcome news to children. It gives them the security of knowing that the "rules" won't change and the hope that they can relate directly to Him.

Yet God exists in three Persons: Father, Son, and Holy Spirit. This is called the "Trinity" or "Three in One." God is a whole—One. That means you can't divide Him into parts. At the same time He is three Persons. Jesus' baptism gives a clear picture of this: Jesus was in the water, the Father spoke from heaven, and the Spirit came down like a dove (Matthew 3:16-17).

Explain that the three Persons have different jobs:

• The Father is the source of everything. He sent His Son. (See John 5:37; 1 Corinthians 8:6.)

• The Son, Jesus, when He was on earth, showed who God is and what He's like. He's your role model and example. He died to save you from your sins. He will judge everyone in the end. (See John 5:22; Romans 5:8; 8:34; Hebrews 1:3.)

• The Holy Spirit helps you get to know God and grow as His child. He guides you into the life God has planned for you. He's with you, teaches you, and gives you gifts to help you do what God wants. (See John 14:16-17, 26; 1 Corinthians 12:4; 2 Thessalonians 2:13.)

Q: When Did God Start?

God is eternal. He created time along with everything else, so it can't have any effect on Him.

What does that mean? God is never rushed! Your children never need to worry about Him running out of time—or disappearing. He is always around—always was, always will be (Hebrews 1:11; Revelation 1:8).

Nothing exists apart from God. Not only did He make everything, but He keeps it going. He is the ultimate source of everything (Acts 17:28; Hebrews 2:10).

To reinforce these truths, try the following:

• Point out to your children that God's qualities all fit together. For example, if God is the only God but not eternal, then something could exist when He's not around—possibly other gods. Or if God did not know everything, how could He do everything? There would be things He wouldn't know how to do! God is either all of these things or none of them.

• Point out that sometimes we try to put God in a box—to make Him small, safe, and completely understandable. But we need to take all the limits off God; there are none! Have your kids go through your home and collect a variety of boxes—shoeboxes, large cartons, lunch boxes, tiny jewelry boxes. Put all the boxes on the floor and ask, "Which of these boxes would God fit into? Do you think He'd like to live in a box? Why might somebody try to keep Him in a box?" Explain that even though God wants to be our Friend, we can't "tame" Him, turn Him into a "pet," or control Him. He's always bigger and more powerful than our words can describe. We can expect life with Him to be full of surprises, to blow us away!

Q: How Does God Feel About Me?

Children need to understand what "God is your loving Father" means in practical terms. You're probably already demonstrating that every loving parent wants to take care of his or her children, guide them, protect them, teach them, help them grow strong and wise, clothe and feed them, give them advice, help with homework, and more.

Explain to your children that God, their heavenly Father, wants all this for them, too (James 1:17; 1 John 3:1). He made them because He wants a loving relationship with them. As you make it clear that God is loving, children will see Him as approachable and want to move closer to Him.

Here are some activities that reinforce those truths:

• When your child needs something, involve God in the equation if possible. For example, if your child asks for a glass of milk, you might mention how wonderful it is that God made cows, and helped people make dairy farms and grocery stores. If your child is worried about a sick pet or having trouble breaking a bad habit, pray together about that.

• At gift-giving times—Christmas and birthdays, for instance—remind your children that every good thing ultimately comes from God and that He enjoys giving it to them. This doesn't mean that human gift-givers shouldn't get credit; it may mean sending thank-you prayers as well as thank-you notes.

• When your children are ill or injured, assure them that God cares—even if He doesn't answer requests for healing right away. You may want to tell the story of how Jesus didn't heal Lazarus immediately, how Jesus cried when He saw how hard the death of Lazarus was on his friends, and how Jesus finally raised Lazarus to life (John 11:1–12:19).

God cares not only what your children are like now but also about the people they're going to be. He cares about what they're going to do with their lives. Assure them that they're special to God, and that He has a plan for their lives that suits them perfectly (Psalm 139:14-16; Ephesians 2:10). Here are a few ways to communicate that idea:

• Most children love to hear stories about what it was like when they were born and what they did when they were babies. When you speak of events surrounding your children's births, include God's involvement in the story. He was not an absentee Father; He was there, involved in their creation and eagerly awaiting their entry into His world.

• Take time to dream about the future with your children. Ask, "What would you like to be when you grow up? How could you help other people in a way that maybe no one else could?" Plant the idea that God has a plan for them. Remind them that God wants them to be all they can be, and He will help them do that.

• You can help children know that both you and God want them, that you're excited they're in the world. You can remind them of this anytime, but birthdays are an especially good time to do so. When you say, "I'm so glad you were born," mention that God is glad, too.

Q: How Do We Know God Made the World?

Your kids need to know that believing in a biblical view of creation is reasonable and based on evidence. Here are just a few faith-building facts you can share with them:

1. Evolutionists generally assume that single-cell creatures slowly changed into fish that crawled onto land and eventually evolved into humans. But even if the earth is four billion years old, as evolutionists say, many scientists realize this is not nearly long enough for even single-cell creatures to develop. Even with enough time, the odds of all the parts of a single-cell creature coming together by themselves in the right way to form life are from 1 in 1,060 to 1 in 1,040,000. And what about a human being, made of millions of cells and many interconnecting systems? The odds are impossible to calculate!

2. There's still no solid evidence of transitional creatures between reptiles and birds and between apelike animals and humans. "Missing link" discoveries have proven false. Some consider Heidelberg man, reconstructed from a jawbone, to be a missing link—but fully human natives of New Caledonia have the same jawbone.

3. Some people think that if God cannot be proven scientifically to exist, then He does not exist and there must be some other explanation for the universe. But even science assumes the existence of unseen subatomic particles simply because of their effects on their surroundings. Isn't it reasonable to believe God exists when His effects can be seen all around us?

4. Chance or creation? Since none of us was present at the beginning, it's a matter of faith either way. Everyone believes "unprovable" things—some more reasonable than others. Based on the evidence, faith in God seems at least as reasonable as the alternative.

As you seek to counter false ideas about God, keep in mind three tips that can make your job easier:

1. Unless they indicate otherwise, assume your children are with you, believing what you've taught them.

2. Avoid force-feeding. Instead, watch for times when children are curious. Give them what they can handle and come back later when they're ready for more.

3. Help children find books, videos, and other resources that offer evidence for the biblical view. Not all the answers have to come directly from you. If children have trouble understanding the resources alone, explore them together.

Q: Why Do People Believe Different Things About God?

As your children internalize what you've taught them about God, making it part of their own belief system, they'll notice that not everyone believes the same things. Friends, teachers, media—all will challenge your children's relationship with God and their understanding of who He is. You can help prepare them for these assaults so they won't be taken by surprise, confused, or deceived.

Your children will meet people who don't believe in God, who believe wrong things about Him, or who follow different religions. You can help them understand why with an explanation like the following:

"Some people don't want to believe in God. Some have seen 'Christians' who didn't act like followers of Jesus. They think, *If that's what believing in God does to you, I don't want it.* Others don't want to believe because they don't like being told what they can or can't do. They like doing as they please and don't want to hear that what they're doing is wrong. Still others simply don't know about Jesus. Or their families have taught them to believe in other religions. We can pray for them—and let them know why we believe as we do."

Kids may find it easy to reject ideas like atheism, but may fall prey to more subtle distortions of who God is. For example, they may get the impression that God is the "eye in the sky," watching and waiting for them to mess up—rather than someone who is on their side, enjoying them and helping them to try again when they fail.

Or they may fall prey to the opposite notion—that God doesn't care about sin and just wants everyone to be happy.

To help children form a balanced, biblical view of God, keep bringing them back to what the Bible says about Him in verses like Romans 6:23; 2 Thessalonians 1:6; 1 John 4:8.

Explain why it's important to believe what the Bible says about God. For example, if Jesus isn't God, He couldn't have been perfect or died to pay for our sins; He would have had to pay for His own. The result: no forgiveness or life in heaven with God after we die.

THE BIBLE

Q: Why Read the Bible?

Why do your children need to know early on that the Bible is God's book? Because it will be so basic to their relationship with Him. It's a one-of-a-kind book that only God could have written. And He wrote it for you and your family!

Children also need to know that God's book is true—not just a storybook like others they look at or have read to them. Except for certain stories, such as parables, the events in the Bible really happened—and the people in it were real.

To see what Scripture has to say about itself, check passages like 2 Timothy 3:16; Psalm 33:4; 119:160; John 5:39; 1 Thessalonians 2:13. To encourage Bible reading as your child grows, try the following:

• As your children start with the simplest board books, give them simple Bible storybooks, too. Let them see your "grown-up" Bible and those of older siblings, explaining what these are and how you enjoy them. Help your toddler look forward to getting older and owning a Bible that has more of God's story in it.

• When possible, choose Bible storybooks that take your children from the beginning (Creation and Adam and Eve) to the end (Jesus' resurrection, the growth of the church, and Jesus' return)—and that introduce the Bible's main characters. This helps youngsters to see that God's Word is not just a collection of unrelated events and people.

• Help young children understand the idea of "true" stories by saying something like, "I'm your Mommy (or Daddy). You're my child, and you live in Mommy's (and/or Daddy's) house. That's a true story." Recount a recent incident involving the child and explain that this, too, is a true story. This prepares children to understand what you mean when you say that the Bible and the stories in it are true.

• If you can tell Bible stories on your own, make the experience fun! Let your children add sound effects (stomping feet for thunder, slapping knees for rain, etc.). Include as much drama and expression in your voice as you can. Older children in this stage may also be able to tell the stories back to you!

• To remind your children that a Bible or Bible storybook is different from other books, approach it differently. Before you open it, try asking God to help you and your children understand what you read. This will also serve as a good model later as they begin to read the Bible on their own.

Once your children know the Bible is God's book, they need to learn why He gave it to them. Let them know that through the Bible they can find out about the God who loves them so much, and about His plan for them. It's their instruction manual for life, prepared by the inventor of life Himself. To make those points, try these ideas:

• It's a love letter! It's an autobiography! It's a history book! It's a true adventure! Refer to the Bible in a variety of ways so that your children can see that it has a number of purposes.

• Bring out the instruction book to your DVD player, camera, or other device. Explain that the book helps you know how the device works best and how to get the most from it. Point out that the Bible is our instruction book for life, written by the One who created us.

• No matter how many Bibles or Bible storybooks you may have in your home, be sure that each child sees a particular one as belonging to him or her. Your children need "personal" Bibles or Bible story-books. This reinforces the idea that God's special book is for them.

• If your Bible storybook doesn't link the stories together, try doing this yourself as you read them. Help children understand the order of the stories—for example, that Adam and Eve came before Noah, who came before Abraham, who came before David, who came before Jesus. This adds to their understanding of the overall story. So does learning the names and order of the books of the Bible.

• Children need to know that even though the Bible is made up of many stories, they add up to the one big story of God's plan for the world from Creation to eternity. That plan: to make it possible for us to be His children. Besides giving your children a context for each story, this helps them find their way around the Bible, thereby making it less likely that they'll be intimidated by "big" Bibles later on.

• Is your child afraid of a bully at school? Read and discuss the story of Daniel in the lions' den (Daniel 6). Is your child refusing to forgive someone? Talk about the parable of the unmerciful servant (Matthew 18:21-35). When your children struggle with stress or character issues, remind them of Bible stories that can help them understand how God wants them to be and behave in those situations. This reinforces how relevant God's Word is and that God cares how they feel and act.

• Let your older child know about an issue with which you struggle—controlling your temper, being generous, trusting God, etc. Show your child how you can look in the Bible (starting with a concordance) to find verses that will help you in that area. Let him or her see you write a few of the verses on index cards; post these where you'll encounter them often. Give children a report every week or so on how God's Word is enabling you to make progress with your problem. At the end of a month, help your children go through a similar process with difficulties they face.

Q: How Can I Read the Bible When It's So Long and Confusing?

It's important to know how Bible stories fit together. Without this, your children will have difficulty keeping Bible events and characters straight or understanding how Scripture as a whole points to Christ.

To sort things out, you can use activities like these:

• Help children learn the order of Bible events with the following game. Write at least 10 of the major events (Creation, the Flood, David's reign, Jesus' birth, Paul's ministry, etc.) on index cards, mix them up, and have kids line them up in the proper order. When children have learned the order of the biggest events, do the same with other events (high points of Jesus' ministry, for example) and characters.

• Try a "sword drill" using a children's Bible or Bible storybook. Call out the name of a story ("Moses and the Burning Bush," for instance) and see whether your children can find it. Do this with several stories, helping as needed. After playing the game several times, children will have improved their grasp of how the stories fit into the Bible's chronology.

• To encourage kids to start searching the Scriptures for themselves, challenge them to find out on their own what the Bible says about a situation they're facing—a rocky friendship, for instance, or a decision about how to spend some money. If they get stuck, help them out. When they're done, ask them to share with you what they found.

• The ancient names of the Bible's countries and cities, even when shown on maps, may seem like imaginary places to your children. Using a contemporary atlas, point out these places on modern maps. Babylon, for example, seems far, far away; Iraq seems much more immediate.

Q: How Do We Know the Bible Is True?

Let your kids know that the Bible we have is exactly what God wanted to give us. God has guarded the Bible over the centuries so that what Christians have is what He wants them to have. For many hundreds of years before the first printing press, Scripture was copied by hand—carefully. We can be sure it is God's Word to us.

As you approach this topic, assume that your children believe the Bible is God's Word. Offering evidence simply preempts doubts and prepares them for the next stage. If your children want evidence for the Bible's accuracy, share the following with them:

• The older the copy we have of something is, the more accurate it probably is—since it was copied from writings that were closer to the original, there were fewer chances for mistakes to be made. There are over 5,000 old, handwritten copies or parts of copies of the New Testament. The oldest is part of the Gospel of John, copied only 20 to 70 years after John wrote it. Imagine, if John had children or grandchildren, they could have seen or touched it! There are also tens of thousands of pieces of copies of the Old Testament. And scholars have the whole New Testament from only 300 years after the last book in it was written! Comparing these manuscripts to today's Bible shows that it hasn't changed in any way that affects what we believe.

• When manuscripts from different places and times say the same things, it shows they were copied accurately. Until 1947, the oldest piece of the Old Testament was from 800 years after Jesus. But the Dead Sea Scrolls were discovered that year; they included a copy of Isaiah from about 200 years before Jesus—a thousand years older than the oldest copy we had—and the two are almost exactly the same!

• The stories about Jesus, the Gospels, were written down less than 50 years after the events happened. Many people who had been there at the time, or their children (who had probably heard the stories umpteen times), would still have been alive. If the stories were wrong, they would have said so!

• To bring home how amazing the Bible's accuracy is, get your children to copy several verses by hand. They're bound to make a mistake or two—and that's only in one small section!

• God used more than 40 people to help Him write the Bible's 66 books. He used their personalities, ways of speaking, cultures, and experiences to write down exactly what He wanted us to have. Some of the people God used were rich; others were poor. They were kings, poets, prophets, generals, priests, farmers, shepherds, fishermen, prisoners—even a doctor and a politician. They lived over a period of 1,500 years, on three continents, and spoke different languages. Yet they all agreed about life, God, and right and wrong! Without God overseeing this process it would have been impossible.

• Over the years, many have doubted the Bible. Since they had no other sources that talked about some of the things in the Bible, they said the Bible was wrong. Then archaeologists began studying old things to learn about the past. They found evidence that confirmed what the Bible said. Here are just two things people doubted and what they found:

What they thought: Moses couldn't have written the first Bible books (Deuteronomy 31:24) because when he lived, no one knew how to write yet. *What they found:* A carved rock from 300 years before Moses with laws written on it, known as the "Black Stele"; tablets from the excavated city of Ebla, written a thousand years before Moses; many other ancient writings.

What they thought: Pontius Pilate wasn't a real person. If he was, he wouldn't have been called "Prefect," as the New Testament calls him. *What they found:* A large stone in Caesarea, saying, "Pontius Pilate, Prefect of Judea."

TOPIC 3

JESUS

Q: Who Is Jesus?

Jesus is God—and human, too. He lived on earth, showing people what God the Father is like. It's a mystery how someone can be divine and human, but with God everything's possible. Because Jesus is God (John 1:1-3, 14), He could live perfectly and pay for our sins; because He is human, He knows from experience what it's like to walk in your children's shoes (Philippians 2:6-7).

The Jesus most children relate to is the Man, their Friend. But they also need to know that He is God, with all the same qualities and abilities as God the Father. He was always alive and with God from before time began. He made everything. When children know that Jesus made everything and therefore knows how it all works, they understand that He knows the very best way to live.

Here are some ways to help your child understand who Jesus is:

• When possible, as you read your children Bible stories about Jesus or talk about Him during the course of a day, try to convey the awesomeness of who He is: God the Son, who has always been, who created everything. For instance, while telling the story of how Jesus fed thousands of people, you might say, "Making a big meal out of a few loaves and fish was no trouble for Jesus—He made all the fish in the ocean!" Or, when talking about how Jesus blessed the children, you could ask, "If you were standing in line to see Jesus, would you be nervous? Do you think those children knew that He is God?" Such side notes of awe, wonder, and respect help your children begin to understand the divine nature of Jesus. It's easy to stop being wowed by who He is and what He did. Remind yourself and convey the "wow" to your children!

• At Christmas, our celebrations often emphasize the human side of Jesus—the vulnerable baby in the manger. If you want to remind your children that Jesus is also God, an Advent calendar may help. As your children open a little door on the calendar each day during December, wonder together what might have been going on in heaven as God's Son prepared to come to earth in human form.

Q: How Do We Know Jesus Is Really God's Son?

We shouldn't be surprised when those who want to undermine Christianity attack Jesus. After all, He's the cornerstone of the Christian faith! Your children will face those who say that Jesus never really lived or that He wasn't really God. You can help prepare them for this by making sure their faith in Him is solidly grounded.

For biblical testimonies from eyewitnesses, see passages like Acts 2:22, 24, 32, 36 and 2 Peter 1:16. But can you "prove" to your children that Jesus really lived? Perhaps not. Still, you can offer convincing evidence. If you like, read the following to them or share it in your own words.

• Eyewitness accounts: The Bible is our main source for information about Jesus. Is the Bible accurate? It's been shown to tell the truth about so much else that you can be confident it tells the truth about Jesus. Those who wrote the Gospels were convinced that what they'd seen and heard was real. Their books were written when others who'd been there were still alive. If the Gospel writers had been telling lies, these others would certainly have exposed them—but they didn't.

• Extra-biblical sources: The Bible isn't the only book that mentions Jesus. Others who wrote not long after He lived show that He was a real, historical person. Flavius Josephus, a Jewish historian who lived around A.D. 70, mentioned Jesus, saying that He was condemned to death by Pilate and then appeared alive again on the third day. Josephus also mentioned Jesus when he told how James, Jesus' brother, was killed. Then there's a letter from a leading Roman, Tacitus (around A.D. 112), mentioning that Jesus was put to death under Pilate. And some Jewish teachers of the time referred to Jesus or Yeshua.

• Jesus claimed He was God. As C. S. Lewis wrote, there are only three things you can believe about Jesus' claim: He is who He says He is (God and Lord); He was a liar who knew He was lying; or He just thought He was telling the truth when He wasn't (in other words, He was a lunatic). Lots of people would agree that Jesus was a great teacher of right and wrong. If He was, He couldn't be a liar. Was He crazy? None of His other words or actions suggest that He was. The only possibility left is that He's who He claims to be—Lord.

• Jesus rose from the dead. Jesus died, yet three days later He was alive again. What happened? The Romans made sure Jesus was dead. His body was wrapped in cloths with spices, which made the grave clothes stick to the body—very difficult to remove. He was placed in a burial chamber cut into solid rock, its one exit covered by a huge stone that took several people to move. Soldiers guarded the tomb; they knew that sleeping on the job brought a death penalty.

Three days later, the tomb was empty. The huge stone had been moved away from the tomb; the grave clothes were empty as if Jesus' body had passed right through them. The soldiers were bribed to say they'd fallen asleep, yet they were not punished for it. More than 500 people saw Jesus alive after His death. And the disciples were never the same, changing from scared people hiding from the authorities to bold people who were willing to suffer beatings and even death. Knowing Jesus rose from the dead helped them to be bold.

• How do we know Jesus is the Messiah? One way is through the predictions that Jesus fulfilled—60 major Old Testament prophecies about the Messiah! For instance, Micah 5:2 predicted that the Messiah would be born in Bethlehem; Genesis 49:10 foresaw that He would be from the tribe of Judah; Psalm 16:10 hinted that He would be raised from the dead.

Q: Why Did Jesus Have to Die?

As one child asked, "Why did Jesus have to die? It isn't fair." Younger children may simply accept without questioning that Jesus died for them. For older kids, questions are more likely.

Most younger children can grasp a very basic story. It might be expressed this way:

"Everyone, even you, does some wrong things. These wrong things are sin and make God sad. But God loves us so much that He sent His Son, Jesus. Jesus died for us so that we could be forgiven and could be God's children. Just as you need to tell me you're sorry when you've done something wrong, you need to tell God you're sorry for doing wrong things and ask Him to forgive you because of what Jesus did. He will. From then on, you are God's child. And if you do anything wrong after that, you can ask God to forgive you and help you do better—and He will."

If your older child wonders why the sacrifice of Jesus was necessary, you may want to share the following:

"Why did Jesus have to die? Well, He didn't have to. He chose to, out of love.

"God loves the world. He wants to have with everyone the kind of close relationship He had with Adam and Eve in the very beginning. The only way to do that was to take care of the sin problem.

"God made people and chose to be their Father. He chose to be responsible for them. Parents pay for what their children break. If parents don't pay, who will? The child usually can't. In a similar way, God made Himself responsible to pay for the thing His children 'broke'—their relationship with Him. He did this knowing what it would cost, because He was a loving Father. If He didn't pay for it, who could? No one.

"The punishment for sin is death. Since everyone sins, everyone would have to pay the death penalty. Only someone who was not born sinful (which excludes everyone since Adam and Eve) could die for others. Everyone else could die only for himself or herself. The only perfect Person is Jesus. He defeated Satan and sin when He died and rose again. This is why Jesus is the only way to God."

To further help your child understand this, try the following:

• Younger children may be baffled by the idea that Jesus "died on the cross," especially if they don't understand what death is. If you sense that a discussion of death would scare your preschooler, rather than inform, concentrate on talking about the love and actions of Jesus, especially the fact that He came to rescue us. When your child is ready to understand what it meant for Jesus to give His life, explain that part of the salvation story.

• Do you use time-outs, spankings, or lost privileges to discipline your child? Try mentioning these as you explain the concept of sin and how Jesus paid the price for ours. Children will understand how wrong acts displease God because they know how you respond when they disobey. Explain that wrong actions put a wide space between your children and God—one that they can't cross alone. That's why Jesus came—to make a way for them to cross back to God and be forgiven. If your children have already accepted Jesus, emphasize that they can go to God anytime, about anything, and ask Him to forgive them when they've done something wrong.

Q: When Will Jesus Come Back?

Children are often drawn to—and confused by—the prophetic parts of the Bible. As they read their Bibles or listen in Sunday school, your children will encounter Ezekiel, Daniel, Revelation, and other sections that are difficult to understand. They may be even more confused when they learn that Christians interpret these writings in different ways. You can help reduce the confusion—and assure your children that the most important thing to know about the future is that God has a wonderful plan for us, a plan that includes the return of Jesus.

"For the Lord himself will come down from heaven, with a loud command, with the voice of the archangel and with the trumpet call of God, and the dead in Christ will rise first. After that, we who are still alive and are left will be caught up together with them in the clouds to meet the Lord in the air. And so we will be with the Lord forever. Therefore encourage each other with these words" (1 Thessalonians 4:16-18).

"Now, brothers, about times and dates we do not need to write to you, for you know very well that the day of the Lord will come like a thief in the night" (1 Thessalonians 5:1-2).

When children ask what prophetic passages mean, use the opportunity to explain a couple of basic guidelines for interpreting the Bible:

• Start with the straightforward. God presented clearly what He really wants us to know. Things about the future that are less urgent to know He presents symbolically. It's better to first read "basic" scriptures that deal with the end times (like Matthew 24:1-5 and 1 Thessalonians 4:13–5:11) and then move to more symbolic passages (such as Revelation and Daniel 7–12), rather than the other way around.

• Look for the big idea. The question to ask about tough passages is, "What's the main point?" The main point of Revelation, for instance, is "Jesus is coming back. Be ready!"

How can you deal with differing views of the end times? Let children know that Christians have various opinions about the meaning of certain scriptures, especially those that contain symbolic language or that don't go into great detail about an issue. Let them know your viewpoint. Help them understand that the principles are more important than the details, and that God's Spirit will help them understand what they need to know. As for prophecy, explain that none of us will completely understand it—until it happens!

SIN AND SATAN

Q: Who Is Satan?

Evil can be an uncomfortable subject. But your children are growing up in a world that's disfigured by the results of sin, and they need to know why. They need to know that Satan is real, that he has power on earth—and that Jesus has ultimately defeated him. They need to know that bad things happen because of sin's side effects, and that Satan has blinded many people to the truth of God's Word.

To help your children understand who Satan is, you may want to share the following:

"A very long time ago an angel named Lucifer rebelled against God. He wanted all the power, to be like God, and to replace God. His sin led to his being thrown out of heaven and sent to earth. Other angels—now demons—chose to follow him. On earth he told the first lie and tricked Adam and Eve into disobeying God, too. That was just the beginning.

"Satan is powerful. But he was created—so he's far, far less powerful than God. He can't create. The Bible calls him a liar and the Father of Lies because he started out with lying and he's still at it. He hates God and anyone who follows God, so he tries to keep people away from Him. He loves evil.

"But don't be afraid. When Jesus died and rose again, Satan's power was broken. For help against him, all a Christian has to do is go to God and ask. Satan hates that!

"Satan is also part of the reason why bad things happen in the world. But people do bad things, too, when they decide their way is better than God's. And every time it leads to trouble!

"God wants people to be free to choose to love Him. So He gave everyone a free will—the ability to make choices. Because people are sinful, they often choose wrong things. Every wrong choice has consequences. Some bad things happen because people make evil or bad choices. God could stop it, but that would mean taking away people's free will. He lets people have what they choose, but He can turn the bad into good to help us grow.

"Other bad things, like death and disease, are a result of sin, too. This doesn't mean that people who get sick are being punished for their sins. It means that when Adam and Eve sinned, it affected every created thing. Because we live in a world where Satan still has power, there is pain and suffering. But the end of the story is clear: Jesus wins!"

When you're talking about the devil and his demons, keep the focus on God. Emphasize that God is in control and has His plan on track. Yes, there's a roaring lion wanting your children to do wrong and to destroy their lives, but Jesus overcame the devil. Your children can overcome, too. If they're afraid of Satan or demons, remind them that Jesus is with them all the time—and He's much stronger than Satan. All they have to do is pray for help. Jesus will keep them safe as they follow Him.

Q: How Am I Supposed to Fight the Devil?

When your children resist Satan by doing things God's way—making right decisions, asking for forgiveness when they sin—it's a victory for the winning side.

Here are some Bible passages that may help your child grasp the idea that there's a spiritual battle going on:

"Submit yourselves, then, to God. Resist the devil, and he will flee from you" (James 4:7).

"Be self-controlled and alert. Your enemy the devil prowls around like a roaring lion looking for someone to devour" (1 Peter 5:8).

Tell your children that when they face temptation it's a good idea to turn to the Bible. When He was tempted, Jesus dealt with the devil's attacks by quoting Scripture. Your children can do what Jesus did—counter the devil's lies with verses they know (or can find) in the Bible, and choose God's way. Encourage them to pray when they're tempted, too—even if they're in the middle of making a mistake. When they ask for help, God will answer.

Reassure your children that even when they've blown it and given Satan a foothold, they can go to God for strength and forgiveness. You can model God's unconditional love by maintaining an open-door policy for your children when they've done wrong. Let them know that you're available for help and forgiveness, not just punishment.

Avoid giving your children the impression that the devil is scary. He's a master deceiver, a master liar. Seeking the truth and following God makes him powerless in our lives. Rather than railing against him (see Jude 9), however, let God judge him. Satan's fate is sealed. He's just trying to cause as much damage as he can before he's thrown into the lake of fire forever.

Q: How Do I Know God Forgives Me When I Do Something Wrong?

When we sin, we should ask God to forgive us—and He will (1 John 1:9).

It's important to teach children that when they willfully disobey you and do something wrong, they need to ask God to forgive them. They also need to ask whoever else was involved to forgive them.

This helps them learn the difference between right and wrong and reinforces their choice to do what is right.

Often children (and adults) can get caught up in making similar mistakes repeatedly. They need to come to a point of conscious choice where they say, "I will not be that way or do that anymore!" Repentance helps them do this.

When they stop for a time-out after bad behavior, talk to them about forgiveness, making the following two points. First, when they repent and ask for forgiveness, they are making a decision to leave that behavior behind and asking God for help to do it right from now on. Second, God wants them to learn to do right because He wants them to have a good life. So when they ask for forgiveness, God instantly forgives them. They start again with a clean slate.

Here are some ways to help your kids understand that concept:

• After correcting your children, show them what they could have done instead. For example, if your child breaks something and denies it or lies about it, explain that you are more upset with the lie than with the fact that the object is broken. Gently tell your child what the proper response would have been—he should have come to you and simply explained what happened. Then you would have had only the accident to deal with, not the issue of the lie.

• Make sure, once you've talked about the sin and prayed about it, that you don't harp on it anymore. Represent God to your kids: Hug them, tell them how much you love them, how pleased you are generally with their behavior, and how pleased you are with how they responded.

• When your children need to ask forgiveness from God, they might be too uncomfortable to pray because they feel so bad. In this case it may be a good idea to offer to pray first. Keep it short and simple: Ask God to forgive them and teach them, and thank Him for some good things about your children that you enjoy.

TOPIC 5

HEAVEN

Q: What's Heaven Like?

Jesus is coming back! The how and when are not as important as the fact of His return. For children, the key is the reason He's returning: to take them to be with Him in heaven forever.

Tell your children that Jesus is getting a wonderful place ready for them, looking forward to the time they will be with Him there. When you teach your children about what's ahead for them in heaven, you give them hope—and the beginnings of an eternal view that puts things here in perspective.

Here are three ways to discuss heaven with your child:

• Read and talk about Bible passages that hint at heaven's wonders. For example: "No eye has seen, no ear has heard, no mind has conceived what God has prepared for those who love him" (1 Corinthians 2:9). See also Isaiah 35:10; John 14:2-3; Revelation 21:3-4.

• People often have the idea that heaven is a boring, static place where nothing ever happens and everyone sits around playing harps. If your children have gotten this impression from TV or other sources, they may wonder, *Why would anyone want to go there?* But heaven will be fantastic! The Bible says there will be no crying, no sadness, no pain or hurt. And heaven isn't just the absence of bad things; the apostle Paul wrote that it's far greater than anyone can even imagine. Next time you and your children enjoy an especially delicious meal, thrilling game, or breathtaking view, point out that heaven is even better.

• If your discussion of heaven brings up questions about angels, explain to your children that angels live in heaven and are God's helpers. They carry out God's plans and sometimes deliver His messages (as Gabriel did to Mary and Joseph), and God has them look after Christians. For more about angels, see Psalm 104:4 and Hebrews 1:14.

TOPIC 6

SALVATION

Q: What Does It Mean to Have a "Relationship with God"?

Jesus died for your children so that their sins could be forgiven. But why? So that they could have a close relationship with God, their heavenly Father!

Make sure your children know that God is eager to have a relationship with them. In the words of John 14:23, "Jesus replied, 'If anyone loves me, he will obey my teaching. My Father will love him, and we will come to him and make our home with him.'"

God wants a special friendship with your kids, one He can have with no one else because each child is one of a kind. In this private relationship they get to know God in their own unique way.

Children need to know that deciding to accept Jesus as Savior is the beginning, not the end. Getting to know God is something exciting they'll be doing for the rest of their lives. Here are some ways to help your kids understand that:

• Let your children see how your relationship with God works. Allow them to hear you pray honestly and conversationally; encourage them to pray the same way, even about things that may seem trivial. Tell them about something God has taught you from the Bible. Talk about times when you've felt especially close to God. If you sometimes feel far from Him, admit it; if it's sometimes hard to relate to a Person who's invisible and doesn't speak to you audibly, admit that, too. Tell them what you would miss most if you couldn't have a relationship with God. As children learn that a relationship with God can be very real even if it has ups and downs, they'll have more realistic expectations as they begin their own.

• Create visual reminders of the relationship between your children and God. Have children draw pictures of themselves hiking with Jesus, for example. Or cut a picture of Jesus from a Sunday school paper and add it to a family portrait. Post these reminders where your children will see them frequently.

Q: Isn't It Unfair to Say That Jesus Is the Only Way to Heaven?

"I can't tell people about Jesus," your children might say. "They'll get mad if I say Jesus is the only Way and their religion is wrong." How can you reply?

Help your children to understand that Christianity isn't exclusive and narrow-minded—it's inclusive and welcoming. "Membership" in most religions is available to a select few—those who perform certain tasks to earn God's favor, who are born into a certain culture, or who otherwise fit a certain profile.

Christianity is the only faith that says you can do nothing to earn heaven—yet your entrance can be guaranteed! Jesus clearly stated the way: "I am the way and the truth and the life. No one comes to the Father except through me" (John 14:6).

This does not exclude people; it includes everyone. No matter where you're from, what you look like, how smart or hardworking or lazy you are, you're welcome. All you have to do is accept God's free gift of forgiveness, delivered to you through Jesus' death. Make sure your children understand that He is the wide-open door to heaven through which anyone can enter and through which everyone must enter. We don't need to "fight" other religions; we just need to tell people the truth and give them the chance to meet Jesus.

• Some children, feeling anxious about whether their friends will go to heaven, may try to pressure those friends into becoming Christians. Encourage your children to be gentle in the way they talk about Jesus. They need to be ready, respectful, humble, and caring. No matter what the other person's response is, he or she deserves to be treated with respect. Each person has a God-given right to choose to follow Jesus or not. Arguments, demands, and pressure don't bring people into God's kingdom; loving them, respecting them, and answering their questions can. Urge your children to trust God to help them tell others about Him, and to leave the results in His hands.

• Even the most enthusiastic child needs knowledge and answers to back up his or her zeal. Show your children where to find Bible verses explaining how to accept Jesus. There are many ways to explain the gospel; encourage kids to tell the story of their journey with Jesus in their own words.

STARTING TO FOLLOW JESUS

Q: What Does God Want from Me?

When kids begin a relationship with God, they're usually responding to His free gift of forgiveness. Since they can't earn their way to heaven, there isn't much talk about behavior at that point.

Eventually, though, the subject comes up. Kids learn that some attitudes and actions honor God—and some don't. Following Jesus, it turns out, involves following His example.

Your child may feel he or she didn't "sign up" for this, or may be overwhelmed by the sheer number of biblical commands he or she hears at church. How can you give your child a handle on what God wants most from those who belong to His family?

Here's one way to look at it—10 things God wants from all of us, and many ways to help kids understand them.

1. *To be good, kind, and loving—as the Father and Jesus are (John 15:12).*

• When your younger children do something wrong, focus on saying and demonstrating what they should have done, not just on what they did wrong. Say something like, "Next time we can do it God's way." Be brief with this process, quickly moving on to hugs and fun things that reinforce your expectation that they will want to follow the example of Jesus.

• For younger children, you'll need to show what it means to be kind, good, and loving. For example, if Marie hits brother Ken on the head, kneel down at Marie's level and give her a brief lesson on the topic of touch. Say something like, "When you touch people, you need to be kind and gentle, like Jesus. If you want to touch Ken, this is how you should do it." Take her hand and help her pat Ken's arm. Explain that this kind of touch makes a person feel happy and loved.

• When talking with your children about being kind and loving, do it in a kind, loving way. It's easy to be harsh when a child has just done wrong, but that doesn't affirm goodness. If necessary, give yourself a few minutes to calm down before speaking. When you do, try to phrase your guidance as positively as you can. For example, affirm that kindness and goodness are part of your family identity: "Because we love Jesus, this is how we act in our family."

2. *To see and think good things (Luke 6:45).*

• When listening to music or watching TV with your children, pause occasionally to ask how they're feeling. Use their answers as a springboard to talk about the way we're shaped by what we see and hear. If they're listening to a sad song and feel sad, point out the connection. Do the same if they're upbeat while watching a happy show. Explain that God wants them to see and hear good things because He loves them and wants the best for them.

• What can you do when your children copy the actions of others who fight or speak rudely? In addition to dealing with the disobedience itself, use the incident as a chance to explain how what we see and hear can convince us to do the wrong things. Conversely, cheer your children on when they imitate positive behavior; point out that God wants us to watch and listen to such good examples.

3. *To learn to share your things with others (Luke 3:11).*

• Brianna is just learning that her doll doesn't cease to exist when she can't see it. Before she can feel comfortable sharing her doll, she needs to know it's still there, even when it's being used by someone else. She also needs to understand that the doll still belongs to her, and that she'll get it back later. A sense of ownership must precede sharing. So for younger children, emphasize two truths: God lets us have nice things, and He wants us to share them with others.

• Rather than forcing your children to share a new possession, give them time to enjoy it first. Once they've played with it, sharing will be easier.

• Try trading and taking turns. It's a good way to introduce sharing. If Christopher and Jonathan are playing with their own spaceships, have them trade for a minute or so. As they learn that the ships don't disappear when out of their hands, and that their belongings will be returned, you can increase the trading time. Or sit with your children and play together, taking brief turns with several toys.

4. *To learn and grow and become like Jesus (John 13:15).*

• "Being like Jesus" could be confusing to your children. Explain that this doesn't mean wearing long robes, walking everywhere, and speaking in parables. They're to pattern themselves after Jesus' character.

• Use stories from the life of Jesus to show children how they need to be like Him. For example, the account of how Jesus touched the leper (Mark 1:40-44) shows that Jesus loved unpopular people and helped those whom others avoided. The story of how Jesus "told it like it was" (Matthew 5:21-48; 11:20-24) shows that He was not afraid to call sin what it really is and warn people about it.

• What would Jesus do? Have children come up with real-life dilemmas they might encounter. For instance, at a friend's house the friend wants to watch a violent video your child knows is off-limits; at school, your child knows who stole trading cards from backpacks at recess. Ask, "What do you think Jesus would do in this situation?

How do you know?" Point out that the answer to the question starts with who Jesus is as a Person—His character—and then is expressed in His actions.

Like physical growth, spiritual growth doesn't happen overnight. It occurs little by little as your children regularly spend time with God and internalize what they learn. It happens as they make right choices—and as they make mistakes and learn from them.

Your children need the comfort of knowing that growth involves mistakes and second tries. Instead of expecting instant perfection, God knows that becoming like Jesus is a process, as are discovering how to write letters, memorizing multiplication tables, and painting pictures.

• Let your children know that you're growing, too—as a person, a parent, and a follower of Jesus. Admit that you make mistakes and that you're learning from them. Treat mistakes—yours, theirs, and other people's—gently. Try to see errors as rungs on the ladder of growth rather than as failures.

• Remember that appearances are not the most important thing. Focus on your children's hearts. Avoid pressuring them to act a certain way when their hearts are far from that; they must take ownership of the right attitude before their actions will mean anything. Pushing children's faith experience past their understanding and beyond their hearts can reduce their Christianity to a matter of performance—which implies that if they blow it, they're failures. Actions are important, but good actions mean the most when they flow from the heart.

• Introduce "stretching" experiences in small steps. For example, instead of trying to teach your children to be good servants by making them sing solos at a nursing home, start by having them help you hand out birthday cards or treats at the facility. Work your way up to having the kids do more as they become comfortable in the unfamiliar environment. Give them small "success experiences" that build their confidence about doing the right thing.

• The Bible contains a wealth of verses about growing spiritually, seeking God, and not giving up. Here are some passages you may want to urge your children to memorize and meditate on: Psalm 25:4-5; 42:1-2; Philippians 2:12-13; 3:7-11, 13-14; Colossians 3:1-4, 5-17; 2 Timothy 2:15; Hebrews 6:1; 12:1.

    5. *For your character to match God's character (Hebrews 1:3).*

• Here are seven key character traits of God that your children need to incorporate into their lives. A motto is included with each trait—a phrase that can help children remember that quality if they copy the words onto posters, jewelry, calendars, or other personal items they'll see frequently.

    1. Truth and honesty (Ephesians 4:15): "God doesn't lie, and neither do I!"

    2. Love and compassion (John 15:17; Colossians 3:12): "My heart's in the right place."

    3. Generosity and selflessness (1 Timothy 6:18): "Something's got to give: me!"

    4. Forgiveness and mercy (Colossians 3:13): "I 4give U."

    5. Trustworthiness and faithfulness (Galatians 5:22-23): "Count on me!"

    6. Justice and impartiality (Matthew 23:23): "Life's not fair, but I try to be."

    7. Holiness (Romans 12:1): "Caution: Set apart."

• Point out character traits at work in everyday life. For example, when your child's best friend decides to hang out with someone else, talk about faithfulness; when a child gets too much change at the store, talk about honesty.

• Spell out the benefits of godly character. For instance, honesty works—it's as simple as that. A person who tells the truth consistently will be trusted; others will want him or her as a friend. In contrast, a dishonest person gets a bad reputation; others stop trusting that person with belongings, secrets, and responsibility. When your children understand the benefits of character, they'll be more likely to choose the right direction because they'll know it works best.

6. *To develop your gifts (Romans 12:6-8).*

• As your schedule and budget allow, encourage your children to try a variety of activities and lessons to help them discover their God-given abilities. Let them explore. When your children show an aptitude for something or enjoy a particular activity, affirm them in that and try to make it possible for them to grow in it.

• Point out examples of people using their talents to serve God. Obvious ones might include those who sing songs about Jesus and those who preach, but don't overlook the rest—the photographer who stirs compassion by taking pictures of famine victims, the cook who prepares meals for visiting missionaries, the attorney who defends the poor, etc.

7. *To develop the fruit of the Spirit (Galatians 5:22-23).*

• Explain to your kids that the fruit of the Spirit is so much more than just being nice. This group of qualities comes from inside, in your children's hearts, and can be developed only in cooperation with the Spirit of God. God's fruit makes relationships work and helps us to become more like Him.

• Pray regularly that God will help your children to grow His fruit. Encourage them to pray this for themselves, and point out when they're making progress. Explain that God doesn't expect us to grow the Spirit's fruit on our own; He is eager to help.

8. *To share your faith (1 Peter 3:15).*

• Explain that sharing our faith is simply telling others what God has done for us—from giving us eternal life to answering our prayers to changing our habits. Your children are "witnessing" whether they're talking about God or not. Their lives speak loudly about who they are and what God means to them. Jesus left His disciples the job of telling everyone about Him and what He did. That's an assignment for you and your children, too.

• To help children get used to the idea of talking about something they believe in, ask them to tell you about a favorite TV show, sport, hobby, or best friend. Note their enthusiasm and lack of self-consciousness. Then explain that sharing our faith is telling what we believe about Jesus and why. We don't need to be experts. We just need a personal, living relationship with God that's worth talking about.

• Before encouraging your children to share their faith, make sure they understand the basics themselves. See the "Romans Road" in Family Time 10 for the salvation message and relevant verses.

• Speak respectfully of nonbelievers so that your children will understand that they need to tell people about Jesus in a loving way. Explain that we need to respect other people's God-given right to decide for themselves, and not be pushy. Praying for others is a great idea, but the choice to accept or reject Jesus is theirs alone.

• If children fear "witnessing" because they might not know the answer to a friend's question, assure them that they don't have to know all the answers. If a puzzling question comes up, they can feel free to say, "I don't know, but I can find out," and get help later from you, a book, or a teacher. Many people aren't convinced by "proofs" or arguments anyway. They want to see Christians who show real love, as Jesus did.

The best way to help your children tell others about Jesus is to help them fall in love with Him. Few have an urge to share knowledge that's strong enough to overcome shyness or fear. But most who are in love find it easy to talk about the object of their affection.

9. *To find and follow His will for your life (Psalm 138:8).*

• Explain that God has a plan—a perfect match for the talents, gifts, and personality He's given your child. How does your child discover that plan? A little at a time! Knowing God's will starts with making right choices day by day. Each day we need to ask God what He has for us to do, then follow Him in that direction. If we're seeking a close relationship with God and are obeying Him, He'll lead us into what we're best suited for—what we'll enjoy and find fulfilling.

• What does it mean to be a success? Do your children think that fame or money should be their goal? Help them see that real success comes from doing what God has designed us to do, even if our specific tasks change from time to time. Point out examples of Christians in your church who are serving God as homemakers, attorneys, artists, janitors—paid or unpaid, well-known or not. If possible, arrange for your children to spend time with a few of these people, finding out how they found their niches and how they continue to seek God's direction for their futures.

• Ask your children, "What do you want to be when you grow up?" You'll probably get job-oriented answers; these are fine, but encourage kids to think "outside the box," too. What do they want to *be*? What qualities do they hope to have when they're adults? Use this activity to remind children that God has a plan for the kind of people He wants us to be—not just for the things He wants us to do.

• How can you help point your children toward the occupation, career, or ministry that's right for them? Encourage them to write down a list of "seeds" they think God may have planted in them—their personality type, talents and gifts, likes and wants. These seeds may give clues to what your children will be most fulfilled by doing one day. In the meantime, let them explore a variety of activities so they can find out what they enjoy and are good at. Urge them to pray for help to make the right choices. Remind them that God promises to give wisdom to those who ask (James 1:5).

10. *To commit your entire life and everything you have to Him (Matthew 10:39).*

• More than once Jesus said it was better to lose your life for His sake than to gain the world. You can help your children see why. Explain that turning their lives over to God is more rewarding than running things on their own, because they can trust Him to take better care of them than they can themselves. Help them know how to do this, too—by surrendering their lives to God every day, even minute by minute when necessary. They can learn to let Him be Lord in reality, not just in name.

• "Losing your life" for the sake of Jesus doesn't always lead to obvious rewards on earth. Be honest about this with your kids. Admit that obeying God can lead to being laughed at, making less money, being misunderstood—even being killed. Balance this with a look at the rewards heaven offers.

• Affirm your children's choices to obey God in the small things—when they choose to forgive a bully instead of getting revenge, when they take homework to a sick friend, when they turn down the chance to watch a forbidden movie. As they learn to surrender to God in the "minor" matters of daily life, they'll find it easier to surrender to Him in the bigger things.

• Some children (and adults) fear that giving God control of their lives will lead to misery. For example, asking God to teach them patience will result in having to endure an itchy rash or a loud-mouthed classmate. Or surrendering to His plan will mean having to go to a land that features rainy weather, slimy food, and a language no one can learn. Assure your children that God is loving and kind. If they need to learn patience, they can trust God to teach them in the best possible way. If God wants to send them somewhere, He'll prepare them. God's goal isn't to ask them to do what they hate the most. He has an awesome plan for them.

Q: Why Should I Obey God?

Your children won't always understand why God says to do something. But if you're teaching them who God is and what His character is like, they'll be more likely to trust that His way is best. Children also need to know that, whether they understand the reason or not, it's vital to obey. Their obedience does not depend on their understanding; He is, after all, God.

• When using Bible stories to show how to live God's way, help your children make the connection between the Bible characters' acts and the results. For example, Joseph was faithful to God. He suffered for a time in prison, but later God rewarded his faithfulness, making Joseph the second-most important man in Egypt.

• It's easy when you're tense or hurried to answer your children's questions with "Because I said so." But this reasoning doesn't help them understand that your instructions are for their own good; it doesn't help them trust you. In the same way, "Because God says so" is inadequate. God doesn't just tell us what to do in the Bible; He often tells us why. If you don't know the why behind a command, look it up—or ask someone who's studied the issue.

• Many children are fascinated by the human body and how it works. Using age-appropriate books, explore with your children the amazingly intricate way in which God has created us—from our infection-fighting blood cells to our self-mending skin. Point out that God knows everything about us because He made us; we need to respect Him and obey Him because He's our Creator.

• Who knows the best way to use a computer, mountain bike, or video camera? The person who designed and made it! Explain to your child that the designer can tell you how everything was meant to work, how to get the most out of that thing, and what not to do with it. As the designer of life, God knows better than anyone else how life works. It only makes sense to abide by His guidelines.

• While following God's instructions does lead to the best kind of life, that kind of life isn't necessarily the easiest kind. Doing the right thing can get us in trouble here on earth. People have, after all, been killed for obeying God. Point out to your children that real success in this life is pleasing God—and we may not see the rewards until we're in heaven.

For your children, turning their lives over to God means agreeing that He knows what's best for them, and that He has a great plan for their lives. It means entrusting their dreams and ambitions to His care (Proverbs 3:5-6).

Q: Why Do I Have to Obey My Parents?

One of the Ten Commandments is to honor mothers and fathers— and honor includes obedience. Children need to know that obedience is not optional. In fact, learning to obey you is a key to learning to obey God.

• Show your children how obedience looks. When you're driving, point out the speed limit sign and how you're obeying the law. When you bring your child to the workplace, explain that you're doing what God wants when you provide for your family. Explain that you need to obey too. You obey God, your boss, and the government because obeying is part of God's plan.

• As children grow older, they need to trust that when you tell them to do something, you have a good reason for it. When they're able to understand, tell them why they have to do something—not "because I said so," but because it will keep them healthy, give them a skill they'll need, and so on.

• Say yes to your children whenever you can. Only say no when you have to—when the issue has to do with safety or growing their character, for example. This reflects God's heart. Ask them to do things that are reasonable and for their good, and be prepared to give them the reasons when they're old enough to understand. This, too, reflects God: Everything He tells us to do is reasonable and for our good. This approach to obedience helps children realize as they grow older that God isn't arbitrary or a killjoy. From your example they will begin to see that God's way is the best way.

• Tempting as it might be to make all your children's decisions for them, it won't prepare them for the future. They need to learn how to tell right from wrong for themselves and how to make godly choices. You can begin this process by giving them "safe" arenas in which to choose. For example, let them decide whether to go to a particular church activity; then discuss their choice. Let them decide whether to study for a test; then discuss the results. To help you determine which choices are "safe" for them to make, take their maturity level and track record into account. Let them know that as they earn your trust, you'll trust them with more and more choices.

Q: Why Is Following Jesus Hard?

"Being a Christian is just too hard!" If your children feel that way, they'll appreciate the truth that we don't have to live the Christian life under our own power (Philippians 1:6). Let them know that their part is mainly to cooperate with what God wants to do in their lives. He's right there, ready to help them become more like His Son.

Point out to children that if they've received Jesus as Savior, God is with them continuously through His Spirit who teaches them from His Word, reminds them of His way, and gives them strength to make the right choices when they ask for it. God is for them, cheering them on, helping them grow to the next step.

• When children do the wrong thing and feel guilty about it, they may wonder whether trying to follow Jesus is a lost cause. Assure them that God is never surprised by our mistakes or sins. If anything, He works to bring these into the open so that we know about them and can deal with them. God is there when we blow it; the best Person to talk to right then is God Himself, as we ask Him to forgive us and to help us obey Him more completely.

• Does teaching your children seem like an overwhelming task? Just as they're not alone, neither are you! The responsibility for training your children spiritually is not solely on your shoulders. You teach them truths about God, modeling those truths as well as you can, and God works them into your children's hearts and lives. It's a cooperative process. Remember that God loves your children, and He knows exactly how to guide them.

• Children may be confused over how much of the Christian life is up to them and how much is up to God. Explain that God doesn't do it all, moving us around and talking through us as if we were a ventriloquist's dummies. God is more like a coach, ready to help us learn how to be and what to do. We can choose to cooperate with Him or not. God helps us love, for instance, but doesn't do it for us. That has to come from our hearts.

Q: Am I Supposed to Hear God Talking to Me?

To whom are your children listening? They probably hear plenty of advice from you, from peers, from teachers, from screens and CD players. But do they hear God's voice?

It's usually a still, small voice rather than an audible one. It takes practice to hear, a willingness to obey, and a turning away from distractions. But God's Spirit wants to guide your children into truth and remind them of Jesus' teaching (John 14:26). You can help your children become more sensitive to His leading as you teach them to listen for His influence on their thoughts as they pray, read the Bible, and hear the counsel of other Christians.

• Have you ever felt God was telling you something through an event, something you read, a sermon you heard, or the words of a friend? If so, tell your children the story. What did you do about the "message"? What was the result?

• Encourage your children to start the day by asking God to guide them. If they expect to face specific problems that day, it's a good idea to ask for specific direction. God may not hand them solutions right away, but they can trust Him to give them wisdom when the time comes.

• To help children understand what it means to "hear God's voice," explain that God can communicate with us in any way He likes. Since His Spirit lives in those who belong to Him, He may sometimes help us to know things in our hearts without our having to hear them through our ears. Since our own thoughts and feelings may confuse us, it can be helpful to talk with a more experienced Christian before acting on the things we believe God has "told" us. One guideline to remember: God doesn't tell people things that disagree with what He's already said in the Bible. If we think God is telling us something, we should compare it with His Word to make sure there's no contradiction.

TOPIC 8

PRAYER

Q: What Good Does Praying Do?

Explain that just as the closeness between you and your children grows as you spend time talking, so closeness to God grows through prayer—which is simply talking to Him. You'll want to mention that prayer has its differences; for instance, it often helps to close your eyes when you do it, to help you concentrate. And prayers often include the words "in Jesus' name" because Jesus is the One whose sacrifice made it possible for us to be close to God.

Let children know that God hears them and wants to help them, just as you hear and want to help (Philippians 4:6-7). But God is much bigger than you are, and He knows best how to take care of them. They can talk to Him about anything; God loves to hear from them, just as you do. And since being close to God is so important, talking with Him needs to go on the list of things we do every day.

Here are several ways to make prayer a vital part of your child's life:

• Let your children hear you pray as often as you can. In addition to mealtimes and bedtimes, try praying at "odd" times—perhaps carrying them from the car to their room as they're falling asleep, or when you encounter a beautiful cloud formation during a walk. As you establish the habit, they'll be more likely to pick it up.

• As much as possible, let praying be easy and enjoyable—even fun! While uncontrollable giggles can spoil a prayer time, feel free to pray about funny things that happened during the day—for example, thanking God that you got to share a "Knock, Knock" joke or see the dog chasing its tail.

• Be yourself! Prayer doesn't have to be formal or use certain words. When you pray with your children, favor words and language that are part of their normal, everyday speech—and yours. Requiring formal, unfamiliar language implies that God is "foreign" and unknowable, and that children must put on an act in His presence. Allow your prayers to reflect your feelings, too; if you're excited, for instance, let it show!

• Try "Ping-Pong Prayers"—you pray something, then the child does, then you do, and so on. Or use "Starter Prayers"—after you and your child compile a list of things to pray for, you give a one- or two-word clue of something on the list and your child prays about it. This progression will comfortably move children toward saying their own prayers.

• How can we talk to someone we can't see? If your children have difficulty with this, help them understand by standing near them and having them close their eyes. Be quiet for a moment. Then ask, "Am I still here when your eyes are closed? How do you know?" Then explain, "It's like that with God. Even though you can't see Him, you'll know with your heart that He is there. You can know He never left because the Bible says He'll always be with you."

• Variety is the spice of a prayer life, too! Even if your main prayer time is always at bedtime, avoid praying for the same things or in the same way every night. Make each night's prayer as relevant to the day's events as possible. Ask your child to pray for your concerns sometimes. Rearrange the bedtime routine occasionally so that prayer isn't just another step toward "lights out." This reinforces the truth that prayer is meant to be meaningful.

• Encourage your children to be themselves with God. There's a difference between respect and the form of respect. Respect is a matter of the heart, not of the words. Speaking in reverent tones and terms might sound respectful, but God sees the heart. He is much more interested in an honest relationship than in a pious-sounding one.

• From time to time, at the end of an uneventful day, talk with your child about the not-so-good things that could have happened that day but didn't—getting sick, falling down on the ice, losing milk money on the way to school, an earthquake, etc. Thank God together that these things didn't happen.

• Let children see your own thankfulness and that you credit your own blessings to God. At mealtime, for example, thank God for more than the food. Modeling gratitude and contentment with what you have gives your children a positive example to follow.

• It's helpful to make prayer itself the first topic of a prayer. Encourage your children to begin by thanking God for hearing them and asking Him to help them pray as He wants them to. This "meeting to plan the meeting" prepares the heart.

Q: What Should I Pray About?

You may be telling your children what to pray about—especially if they have trouble coming up with ideas. Try to make a gradual transition, however, to letting them decide what to talk to God about. Help them make a list by asking questions or making suggestions. Eventually they'll be able to make their own list with a little help. This transfer of responsibility helps them see that this is their relationship with God, not yours.

• Children often need help thinking of topics to bring before their heavenly Father. You can lift them out of the "God bless everybody" rut by sharing the following list with them:

1. *Thank-you prayers.* Show appreciation for who God is and what He's done.

2. *Prayers about God's kingdom.* Pray that you—and everyone, everywhere—will do what God wants. Ask that other people will come to know Jesus and that Jesus' church will grow strong so it can do its job.

3. *Leader prayers.* Pray that leaders and those in authority (even teachers and babysitters) will obey God.

4. *Personal requests.* Pray about your own needs and concerns— for health, protection, friendship, etc.

5. *Growing prayers.* Confess wrongs and ask for forgiveness; pray about becoming a stronger Christian.

6. *Prayer for others.* Ask God to help friends, family, and anyone else with needs.

7. *Guidance prayers.* Pray for God to lead you, to help you make the best choices.

8. *Praise prayers.* "Cheer" for God because He's your Creator, and because He has the power to answer all your other prayers!

• Sometimes children don't know how to express their fears, sadness, or even joy in their prayers. Assure them that God can help them know what to say. And because God understands what's in their hearts, He knows how they feel even if all they can do is sigh or cry.

• After prayer, instead of rushing straight to good-night kisses or some other activity, try having a short period of quiet. This reinforces the fact that God is there and that we need to listen in case He wants to give us wisdom on how to deal with an issue we've prayed about. Avoid implying that children should expect audible answers, but assure them that God responds in His way and time.

• Use your children's questions and frustrations as an opportunity to teach them how to ask for God's wisdom (James 1:5; 3:15-17). If they're upset about not being able to take a toy apart or put it back together, remind them that God is ready to help. Show them how to stop and be still for a moment while they ask God for wisdom. Help them think through their situation and watch the ideas come. If God seems to lead them to ask someone else for help, that's fine. God provides us with wisdom in many different ways and on His schedule.

Q: Why Doesn't God Answer My Prayer?

Do your children wonder why they don't always get what they ask for in prayer? You may want to offer an explanation like the following:

"If you ask me at your age, 'Can I borrow the car?' you'll get an automatic no. If you ask, 'Can I do my homework?' you'll probably get an automatic yes. If you ask, 'Can I play with my friend?' the answer will depend on what's best at the time.

"Prayer is like that. Some prayers get an automatic no. For example, Saul (Paul) wanted God's help to persecute Jesus' followers. The answer was no. Prayers to get away with stealing or to help you get back at someone will get a no because God won't help you do something wrong.

"Other prayers get an automatic yes. For example, a prayer for forgiveness, to understand the Bible, to become more like Jesus, to find a way to help someone else, for courage to tell someone about Jesus— all these get a yes. After all, God tells us to pray for these things!

"Then there are the less clear prayers, the ones the Bible isn't specific about. These might get a yes, a no, or a 'wait.' For example, you might pray, 'Help me make the team,' or 'Please give me a bike for my birthday,' or 'Please make Jenny want to be my friend.' The best thing to do when we pray about these things is to ask that God will work them out in the way that pleases Him most. That's what people mean when they pray for God's will. Then, whatever the answer is, you'll know it's what's best for you.

"Sometimes God says no to a request because we're disobeying Him or fighting or not forgiving. He may put our request 'on hold' until we deal with that issue. In any case, God hears every prayer, and He answers according to what's best for us."

Here are some additional ways to handle the question of seemingly unanswered prayer:

• Since they think in concrete terms, children don't always make the connection between their prayers and God's answers. Nor do they always link God with the wonderful things they have. Encourage your children to make a list of their Top 10 favorite things; point out that these are gifts from God. If you keep a prayer list, help children to keep track of God's answers, too.

• A best friend moves away; a beloved pet dies; a bully rules the playground. Your children have prayed about these things, but God hasn't granted their requests. How can you help them deal with the disappointment? Bring them back to the fact of God's love. God cares about their feelings, but He also knows what's best. He wants us to keep praying and not give up. Timing is in His hands, as are the answers. We may not like or understand them. The hard truth is that God wants our faith to grow strong and to be focused on the right things—His love and care—and not on getting what we want or having a smooth life. You can begin this process together, starting with your example as you learn to accept what God sends and allows (Romans 5:3-5).

• Try the following one day at lunch or dinner. Bring out a pathetic-looking meal, perhaps a couple of crackers on a plate. Say, "I'm going to give you a choice. You can eat this now, or you can wait 20 minutes. If you wait, I have something better planned—but I won't tell you what it is." Let kids decide whether to wait. For those who do, serve a favorite food 20 minutes later. Use this as an object lesson to reinforce the truth that sometimes God makes us wait because He has something far better planned.

• As you learn to trust God during tests and trials, be honest with Him and with your children. Show them in the Psalms how David swung back and forth between frustration and praise, reinforcing the truth that it's okay to express your real feelings to God. It's also important to come back to trusting Him, as David did.

• Ask your children to list all the junk food they think they could eat in a single day. Then ask them whether it would really be a good idea. Explain that even though eating a lot of junk food might feel good, it would hurt them in the long run. In the same way, God knows that some of our requests might make us happy for a while but would end up hurting us. Assure your children that God cares about how they feel, but He knows the big picture, too.

• If you've been disappointed by seemingly unanswered prayer, it may be difficult for you to assure your children that God can do anything. You may worry that you'd be setting them up for disappointment, too. Let your children know that you are learning to trust God. Go to the Bible with them and look up verses about God's attitude toward our requests (John 15:7; Romans 8:26). Discuss your feelings with a pastor or mature Christian friend if you like.

CHURCH

Q: Why Do I Have to Go to Church?

Church is God's idea, and for good reason! It's meant to be part of every Christian's learning and support system (Hebrews 10:24-25).

You can encourage your child to be an active, enthused part of the Body by working the following activities into your routine:

• To show your children that church is vital, involve them in it at the earliest possible age. Take them to Sunday school; make sure they're comfortable and secure. If your children have trouble staying when you leave, remain and help if you can for the first time or two. Help them enjoy being there so that they'll gain a positive view of church. As soon as your children can understand, tell them why you go to church: to learn about God, to celebrate His greatness, and to be with others who love Him.

• Get involved in what your children are doing at church. Sit in on some of their classes, helping out if you can. Watch to see that they're learning basic lessons about Jesus through songs, stories, and fun. Encourage them to participate in crafts, games, and action songs, and to answer questions when they're able. Try to bring them together with church friends for playtimes, sending the message that it's important and fun to spend time with Christian friends.

• Whether your church meets on Sunday morning or at another time, try to make that part of the week special. Create fond memories for children to associate with church time—a favorite breakfast, a simple quiz in the car, a picnic. Plan ahead to avoid rushing. Talk with enthusiasm about what you'll be doing at church, and afterward discuss positively what you learned.

• You can't choose your children's friends; after all, they may not click with the same personality types you do. But you can choose the environment from which they take their friends. Make it easy for them to spend time with Christian children. Drive them to church events, have Christian children over, encourage return visits.

• Explain that the Church is people. It's a community of Christians who meet to learn about God, encourage one another, grow, and worship. God knew you and your children wouldn't be able to follow Him alone, so He gave you the Church. Jesus is the head of the Church. It's His "bride." That means He's responsible for it. He loves His church and watches over it to make sure it benefits His children—including yours.

• To help children see how church relates to their lives as a whole, make a point of mentioning church during the week. For example, recall something you heard during a sermon and explain how it might help you resolve a problem you're facing. Get together with another church family. Pray together about concerns listed in the church bulletin. Have a family meeting to decide how much to donate to a special church offering and how each family member might get involved.

• Avoid simply going to church and leaving as quickly as you can. Stick around to talk with other adults and to meet the children in your kids' classes. Use this time to make connections for yourself and for your children. Finding friends at church is a key to feeling part of it all. As your children get to know others at church, they'll feel an increasing sense of belonging and a desire to be there.

• On the way to church, pray together as a family that God will help you learn about Him and develop relationships in which you can both provide and receive support. On the way home, discuss what you learned. Rather than simply asking, "What did you do in Sunday school?" try to be specific. Ask whether your children had fun, what songs they sang, whether they learned anything surprising, what the Bible story was, and how the lesson might help them during the coming week.

• To help older kids understand how worship works, tell them about the "Worship Loop": Worship is like a loop, a circle. It starts with God. We learn about God and realize we can trust Him: He keeps His promises, knows everything, can do anything, is everywhere, and always loves us. That makes us feel like praising and thanking Him and trusting Him with more of our lives. When we let Him take charge of more of our lives, He changes us, making us more like Jesus. When that happens, our praise comes from even deeper inside. We get together with others and tell how wonderful God is. This helps our trust in Him get even stronger, which leads us to greater worship. And on it goes; we get closer to God and worship Him more, which brings us even closer.

• When your children join you in your adult worship service, try to emphasize attitude over outward conformity. For example, if your church has a long worship service, kids might not be able to concentrate and participate the whole time. If their concentration is dwindling, suggest that they ask for God's help to focus; then they can sit quietly and wait, without distracting others. It's far better for them to worship from their hearts for five minutes than to just go through the motions for an hour. In addition, encourage them to worship along with the songs that are meaningful to them. If some lyrics are over their heads, tell kids that they may sit or stand quietly during those songs and talk to God in their hearts. After the service, explain the lyrics so that children can join in next time.

• Point out that your children aren't just the church of tomorrow. They're the church of today! You can help them see your church as their church and find a place to be involved. Kids don't have to wait until they grow up to be supportive of pastors and other leaders, or to give time, money, and energy to God's work.

• If your kids are having trouble fitting in, talk with their Sunday school teacher or the person in charge of children's ministry at your church. Ask whether there are opportunities in the church's program for kids to get to know each other, perhaps in a club program, summer camp, or service project. Meet parents in your church whose children are in your kids' age range; invite these families over for dinner or another activity.

• Are you enthused about church? Do you have a sense of belonging? Chances are that your children can tell whether church is a labor of love for you—or just labor. Expecting them to get fired up about something that leaves you cold is unrealistic. If that's the case with you, take the same steps for yourself that you'd take with your children. Find a spot to serve that taps into your gifts and passions. Join a small group that contains potential friends for you. As you gain a sense of belonging, your children will be more likely to think the same is possible for them.

Q: Why Should I Put Money in the Offering?

God owns absolutely everything (Psalm 24:1). He made it all! But He gives it to you and your children to use and manage for Him. That's the job of a steward.

When you tell your children that everything they have belongs to God and that they're just stewards of it, get specific: toys, clothes, games, videos, books, money, the natural world around them. They're also stewards of their abilities, time, energy, minds, hearts, relationships with God and people, and hopes for the future. All of these are gifts from God. How should they use these gifts? The way God has shown them to through His example: generously, selflessly, wisely.

How can you cultivate a giving attitude in your kids? Try these ideas:

• Children may resist sharing if they're worried about not having enough left for themselves. Explain that when they obey God by sharing, they don't have to worry about running out. It's God's job to take care of them. Their faith and trust in His care are shown by their willingness to give back to God and to help others.

• Are you starting to give your children an allowance? If so, it's a good time to teach them why you give to the church. Explain that you give some of your money back to God as a thank-you for all the wonderful things He's given you. Giving to the church is also a way to show God that you trust Him to look after your needs—and it helps to get God's work done.

• Most older children can easily understand what it means to be "stewards" of God's creation—taking care of the environment, not wasting water or other resources, keeping the world clean by not littering, etc. Explain that this applies to all the things God has given us.

• Teaching children to be good stewards teaches them other spiritual truths, too. For example, tithing teaches them to be thankful for God's care and to value God's church and the Christian community. Giving to missions teaches them their responsibility to reach those who don't know Jesus.

Q: How Come Churches Don't All Agree?

God lets His people serve Him and express their worship of Him in different ways. Your children will encounter variances among churches, and may wonder why. You can help clear up the confusion and guide children to appreciate the freedom God gives us in honoring Him (see Ephesians 4:3-6).

Here are some ways to do that:

• Christians generally agree on the basic doctrines of the Apostles' Creed. If your child is old enough, share this statement of faith with him or her and talk about it.

The Apostles' Creed

"I believe in God, the Father almighty, creator of heaven and earth. I believe in Jesus Christ, His only Son, our Lord. He was conceived by the power of the Holy Spirit and born of the Virgin Mary. He suffered under Pontius Pilate, was crucified, died, and was buried. He descended into hell. On the third day He rose again. He ascended into heaven and is seated at the right hand of the Father. He will come again to judge the living and the dead. I believe in the Holy Spirit, the holy Christian church, the communion of saints, the forgiveness of sins, the resurrection of the body, and life everlasting."

• You can help your children distinguish the essentials of the Christian faith from the way Christians express and celebrate that faith. Explain that God made people with a great variety of personalities and tastes. Naturally, this comes through in how Christians serve and worship Him. Some churches emphasize certain parts of the Christian life—sharing one's faith, studying the Bible, helping the poor, etc. Churches also tend to emphasize certain forms of worship, based on tradition and preference—choosing one kind of music over another, dressing in a particular way, moving or not moving to show their feelings, etc.

• Try taking a family field trip to a church unlike your own, so that your children can experience another form of worship. Then ask, "How might the things they did be expressions of their love for God? How is that church like ours?"

• It's important to focus on the things Christians have in common. But feel free to teach your children about the things that make your church unique too, so that they can fully participate in your worship service and the rest of your church's program.

NOTES

Part I

1. Statistics attributed to Nazarene Church Growth Research and the International Bible Society, cited at http://home.snu.edu/~HCUL BERT/ages.htm.
2. "Evangelism Is Most Effective Among Kids," October 11, 2004, found at www.barna.org.
3. From the "Walk Away" Web site sponsored by the Institute for First Amendment Studies (gemini.berkshire.net/~ifas/wa/stories.html).
4. National Aeronautics and Space Administration, found at http://www.nasa.gov/returntoflight/launch/countdown101.html, p. 3.
5. Craig and Janet Parshall, *Traveling a Pilgrim's Path* (Wheaton, Ill.: Focus on the Family/Tyndale House Publishers, 2003), p. 11.
6. Ibid., p. 12.
7. Mindy Stoms, "Making It Personal: Jesus Loves Me!" July 13, 2007. Found at TodaysChildrensMinistry.com, p. 1.
8. Ibid., p. 2.
9. *Parents' Guide to the Spiritual Growth of Children*, John Trent, Rick Osborne, and Kurt Bruner, eds. (Wheaton, Ill.: Focus on the Family/Tyndale House Publishers, 2000), pp. 301-302.

Part III

1. Adapted from Rick Osborne, K. Christie Bowler, and John Duckworth, *Parents' Guide to the Spiritual Growth of Children* (Wheaton, Ill.: Focus on the Family/Tyndale House Publishers, 2000), pp. 277-384.

Note: Listing of Web sites does not constitute endorsement or agreement by Focus on the Family with information or resources offered at or through those sites.

FOCUS ON THE FAMILY®

Welcome to the family!

Whether you purchased this book, borrowed it, or received it as a gift, we're glad you're reading it. It's just one of the many helpful, encouraging, and biblically based resources produced by Focus on the Family for people in all stages of life.

Focus began in 1977 with the vision of one man, Dr. James Dobson, a licensed psychologist and author of numerous best-selling books on marriage, parenting, and family. Alarmed by the societal, political, and economic pressures that were threatening the existence of the American family, Dr. Dobson founded Focus on the Family with one employee and a once-a-week radio broadcast aired on 36 stations.

Now an international organization reaching millions of people daily, Focus on the Family is dedicated to preserving values and strengthening and encouraging families through the life-changing message of Jesus Christ.

Focus on the Family Magazines

These faith-building, character-developing publications address the interests, issues, concerns, and challenges faced by every member of your family from preschool through the senior years.

| Focus on the Family **Citizen®** U.S. news issues | Focus on the Family **Clubhouse Jr.™** Ages 4 to 8 | Focus on the Family **Clubhouse™** Ages 8 to 12 | **Breakaway®** Teen guys | **Brio®** Teen girls 12 to 16 | **Brio & Beyond®** Teen girls 16 to 19 | **Plugged In®** Reviews movies, music, TV |

FOR MORE INFORMATION

 Online:
Log on to www.family.org
In Canada, log on to www.focusonthefamily.ca

 Phone:
Call toll free: (800) A-FAMILY (232-6459)
In Canada, call toll free: (800) 661-9800

More Great Resources
from Focus on the Family®

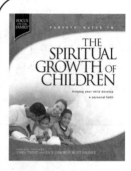

Parents' Guide to the Spiritual Growth of Children
General Editors: John Trent, Ph.D., Rick Osborne, Kurt Bruner

Passing on a heritage of faith to children is an incredible privilege God gives to parents. And now there's a tool to help make it easy! Dozens of simple, practical ways are provided to develop Christian values and make faith in God part of your child's life. Paperback.

Your Child DVD Parenting Seminar: Essentials of Discipline
Hosted by Dr. James Dobson

Get proven answers on one of the biggest challenges parents face with their kids: discipline. This innovative DVD set explores the *Essentials of Discipline* using up-to-date research. With humorous animated vignettes, "mom (and dad) on the street" interviews, and practical teaching, lessons from Dr. James Dobson have never been this fun! 3 DVDs plus parent's guide, approx. 230 minutes.

Creative Correction
Lisa Whelchel offers creative solutions for parents who are out of ideas and desperate for new, proven approaches to discipline. In addition to advice on topics such as sibling conflict and lying, Whelchel offers a biblical perspective and down-to-earth encouragement to parents who are feeling overwhelmed. Paperback.

FOR MORE INFORMATION

 Online:
Log on to www.family.org
In Canada, log on to www.focusonthefamily.ca.

 Phone:
Call toll free: (800) A-FAMILY
In Canada, call toll free: (800) 661-9800.